——— FILIPPO BERIO ———
THE LOW-CHOLESTEROL
OLIVE OIL COOKBOOK

FILIPPO BERIO
THE LOW-CHOLESTEROL
OLIVE OIL COOKBOOK

Sarah Schlesinger & Barbara Earnest

EBURY PRESS LONDON

Published in Great Britain by Ebury Press
an imprint of the Random Century Group
Random Century House
20 Vauxhall Bridge Road
London SW1V 2SA

Second impression 1991

British Library Cataloguing in Publication Data
Schlesinger, Sarah
  The Berio low-cholesterol olive oil cookbook.
  1. Food : dishes using olive oil – Recipes
  I. Title II. Earnest, Barbara
  641.6463

ISBN 0–7126–4806–2

Editor: Jenni Fleetwood
Designer: Gwyn Lewis
Typeset in Century Old Style by Textype Typesetters, Cambridge
Printed and bound in Great Britain by Clays Ltd, St Ives plc

CONTENTS

FOREWORD

It is always a pleasure to spread good news and the 'heart disease story' – which too often seems to be filled with what might be perceived as negative or kill-joy messages – at last has some ingredients which are both sensible and encouraging.

The Family Heart Association, which was established in 1984 by families concerned about the effects of high cholesterol, has consistently sought to discover and highlight foods which contribute to a healthy diet and, in particular, those which help to lower blood cholesterol.

Too often the idea of sensible eating has been portrayed as existing outside the experience of most people. The truth is that the majority of families have a 'repertoire' of meals which are repeated on a weekly or fortnightly cycle; it is through bringing change within that repertoire that heart disease will be prevented. It is for this reason that the Family Heart Association has adopted its policy of 'the sensible alternative'. It not only actively encourages families to experiment and explore dishes outside their normal range of experience but also aims to persuade families to adopt 'the sensible alternative' in preparing the meals which they regularly serve and enjoy.

It would be foolish, for example, to imagine that British people would suddenly lose their affection for fatty foods, or throw away their frying pans. The truth is that the use of animal (saturated) fats in a variety of forms in cooking has become so ingrained in our lifestyles that to bring about change requires a sensible and acceptable alternative. The good news is that such an alternative exists. For centuries it has been known that olive oil 'is good for you' – and the Mediterranean diet has borne witness to that fact. Now, however, we have scientific evidence which demonstrates clearly that monounsaturated fat – which olive oil contains – reduces cholesterol and therefore helps to prevent heart disease. This is good news which the Family Heart Association is delighted to spread. The recipes contained in this book will be of great assistance to the growing number of people who are hearing and responding to our message: 'Help Yourself to a Healthy Heart'!

Don W. Steele
Director, Family Heart Association

THE HEALTH STORY

A century ago, an Italian physician named P. E. Remondino stressed the value of olive oil as an antidote for shrivelled livers, mummified skin, constipation and pessimism. As we learn more about the role of olive oil in helping to lower the risk of coronary heart disease, it becomes increasingly clear that we should have paid better attention to some of his advice.

Nutritionists are constantly seeking improved ways to put our cholesterol and fats in better balance by using natural adjustments in diet and lifestyle that don't require drugs and other forms of medical intervention. The renewed interest in olive oil is a byproduct of this investigative process.

In order to understand the importance of turning to monounsaturated olive oil as our primary source of fat calories, we first have to examine the role of cholesterol and fats in our diets.

The role of cholesterol in cardiovascular disease

Coronary Heart Disease (CHD) kills 180,000 people a year in the UK, 80,000 of them women. This means one in three British men and one in four women are likely to fall victim to this disease. Although some risk factors for this disease such as sex, age and family history are beyond our control, others such as diet, smoking, blood pressure, weight, physical activity and blood cholesterol levels are not. Over eleven million Britons (one in five) are estimated to have dangerously high cholesterol levels. Coronary specialists have predicted that 30 to 50 percent of the potential victims of heart disease could be helped by lowering these levels.

Cholesterol is a white, waxy, tasteless and odourless substance produced by our liver and intestinal tract and is also found in foods of animal origin. We will be using the term 'cholesterol' to refer to the total amount of cholesterol in the blood. The cholesterol in our bloodstream is measured in millimoles per litre, or mmol/l.

Some cholesterol is necessary for making essential body substances such as cell membranes, bile acids and sex hormones and performing other important bodily functions. Without cholesterol we could not stay alive. However, too much can be dangerous since cholesterol contributes to the build-up of fatty deposits on artery walls that can lead to heart attack and stroke.

Our cholesterol can be too high because of diet, lifestyle or family history; 100,000 people in the UK are victims of hypercholesterolaemia, a genetic condition which means that their bodies manufacture more cholesterol than they need. The amount of dietary cholesterol and saturated fats consumed in the food we eat each day can also contribute to elevated blood cholesterol.

Dietary cholesterol is found in foods of animal origin such as egg yolks, red meat, offal and dairy products. Plant foods, including fruits, vegetables and grains such as oats, do not contain cholesterol. Saturated fats are usually of animal origin and are solid at room temperature. Foods high in saturated fat include beef fat, lard, butter, cheese and whole milk, as well as the three tropical oils: palm, palm kernel and coconut oil.

Since cholesterol and fat are not soluble in water, they connect with proteins and travel through the body as lipoproteins. Two major kinds of lipoproteins deserve special attention: low-density lipoprotein (LDL), often called 'bad' cholesterol, and high-density lipoprotein (HDL), often called 'good' cholesterol.

LDL is responsible for depositing cholesterol in tissues. The more LDL in the bloodstream, the greater the chances of its building up and attaching itself to the artery walls.

One role of HDL is to *prevent* the deposit of cholesterol on the artery walls. Consequently, the more HDL and the less buildup of cholesterol there is in the body, the lower the risk of developing heart disease.

However, when there is either very little HDL or too much LDL, the interior lining of the blood vessels can become clogged.

LDL is accompanied on its journey through the body by a special protein called 'apolipoprotein B' or 'Apo B'. Apo B is a tough insoluble substance that tends to adhere to artery walls. Gradually LDL cholesterol and Apo B build up to form a material known as 'plaque'. Since arteries are only 2mm ($1/12$ inch) in diameter in some spots, a very small amount of plaque can narrow an artery. The process of plaque formation is called atherosclerosis.

As the result of atherosclerosis, coronary arteries can become increasingly narrow and less able to expand and contract. When an artery becomes totally clogged, blood flow decreases and the heart muscles start to suffocate. Chest pain or a heart attack may result. Two thirds of deaths from CHD in the UK are caused by the narrowing of these arteries that supply blood to the heart.

High blood pressure may also result when the heart must work harder and harder to send blood through narrow arterial openings. High blood pressure can be both a cause and a warning of heart attack or stroke.

As we follow this chain of events, we can clearly see the importance of having a low LDL level and a high HDL level. The lower your ratio of HDL to total cholesterol, the better. For example, in men, the suggested ratio of HDL to total cholesterol is below 4.6. Some steps that can help you achieve and maintain a desirable HDL level are:

1. Substitute olive oil for the saturated fats in your diet. American research indicates that monounsaturated oils such as olive oil are more protective of HDL levels than polyunsaturated fats such as corn oil. Olive oil reduces total cholesterol without lowering HDL.

2. Eat more seafood. Omega-3 fatty acids in oily fish such as salmon, mackerel, sardines and yellow-fin tuna can boost HDL levels.

3. Add beans, oat bran, apples and other foods high in soluble fibre to your diet. Eating 200 g (7 oz) of dried haricot beans each day can improve the HDL total cholesterol ratio by 17 percent. 40 g (1$^{1}/_{2}$ oz) of dry oat bran daily can boost HDL by up to 15 percent in several months.

4. If you are heavy, lose weight. Getting rid of excess weight raises HDL. However, losing weight if you are already at your recommended level will not boost HDL.

5. Participate in a regular exercise programme. Aerobic exercise has been found to elevate HDL levels in addition to burning calories.

6. Don't smoke. As early as 1970, it was reported that cigarette smoking lowered the blood levels of HDL.

7. If you take vitamins, check with your doctor or nutritionist for advice on which supplements might adversely or positively affect HDL levels.

Finding out about your own cholesterol level

Although cholesterol tests are now available from chemists and health fairs, it is important to be tested under the supervision of a doctor. You will be required to fast for 12 hours before your blood test, and the analysis of the results should include LDL and HDL levels as well as total cholesterol levels.

Although a cholesterol level of below 5.2 mmol/l is deemed acceptable, 5.2–6.5 mmol/l is considered moderate and upwards of 6.5 mmol/l is held to be high, many individual factors such as age, sex, heredity and lifestyle need to be evaluated by your doctor to determine the correct level for you.

If your doctor determines that your cholesterol is in the desirable range, he will probably suggest that you maintain a diet and exercise strategy designed to promote low cholesterol levels. If you have an elevated cholesterol level, he will recommend a cholesterol and fat-restricted diet. If the level is persistently above 6.5 mmol/l, drugs may have to be considered. Even if drugs are taken, a cholesterol and fat-modified diet must still be followed.

The Family Heart Association (FHA) recommends that we reduce out total fat intake to no more than 30 percent of our daily diet. But merely reducing the quantity of total fat in our diet is not enough. We also have to become familiar with the three kinds of fat and learn to include the correct percentage of each type in our daily food plan.

Facts about fats

Fats are vital to good human nutrition. In addition to providing energy, fat contributes to a feeling of fullness, adds taste to foods, acts as a carrier for the fat-soluble vitamins A, D, E and K, and furnishes essential fatty acids that are needed for life and growth.

Fats don't exist in an isolated form, but rather have to be extracted from the foods in which they are found. Butter is removed from cream by churning, lard is removed from animal tissues by heating, and vegetable oils are separated from seeds, nuts, or fruits by pressing or using chemical solvents. Soy, corn, peanut, cottonseed, sunflower, coconut, palm kernel, safflower, sesame and rapeseed oils are extracted from plant seeds, while health promoting olive oil and harmful palm oil are derived from the actual pulp of the fruit.

The terms saturated, monounsaturated and polyunsaturated are used to classify fats. Saturated fats are solid at room temperature. Both monounsaturated and polyunsaturated fats are called unsaturated fats and are liquid at room temperature.

All fats are a blend of saturates, monounsaturates and polyunsaturates. But the proportions vary greatly. Olive oil contains a higher amount of monounsaturated fat than any other oil.

Although past attempts to lower cholesterol in the diet have centred on foods that contain polyunsaturated fats, recently the focus has been shifting to the significance of eating more monounsaturated fat. This new attention to monounsaturates has been prompted in part by concerns about the other long-term health effects of consuming large quantities of polyunsaturated fats. While humans have been eating large amounts of monounsaturated fat in the form of olive oil for thousands of years, the consumption of large quantities of polyunsaturated vegetable oils is relatively recent. No population has existed for a long period of time on a diet in which polyunsaturates provided as much as 8 – 10 percent of its calories. In other words, there is no recorded experience from which to evaluate the consequences of long-term consumption at this rate. In addition, monounsaturated fats are naturally synthesized by the human body while polyunsaturated fats are not.

Some scientists are concerned that the highly reactive nature of polyunsaturated fats can cause them to oxidize and form carcinogenic compounds. Recent research has shown that high doses of polyunsaturates can promote cancer in laboratory animals, dramatically alter cell membranes, and may increase the risk of gallstones.

Research on the dietary benefits of monounsaturates

An early hint at the value of monounsaturates came from the Seven Countries Study, begun in 1958, when researchers tracked various risk factors in healthy middle-aged men including diet, blood pressure, weight, cigarette smoking and exercise habits. When they correlated the data with the men's subsequent rates of heart disease, they discovered that the more saturated fat there was in a diet, the higher the mortality from heart disease. The Finns fared worst, followed by the Americans. The Greeks, Italians and Japanese fared best. Since the Japanese ate very little fat in their diets, their results were not surprising. But unexpectedly the Greeks and Italians had less heart disease even though they consumed a high-fat diet. Most of their fat consumption was in the form of monounsaturated olive oil.

The Seven Countries Study continued over a fifteen-year period as people in traditional olive oil areas began to imitate the tastes of the more affluent populations of northern Europe and the United States. This resulted in their eating more meat and dairy products and cutting back on their olive oil intake. Some researchers noted an alarming increase in the concentration of cholesterol in the blood serum of the men in the Mediterranean area and saw many more coronary patients towards the end of the study.

During the 1980s, Dr. Scott M. Grundy, director for the Center for Human Nutrition at the University of Texas Southwestern Medical Center, and his associate, Dr. Fred H. Mattson, of the University of California at San Diego, became involved in studying the role of monounsaturates in human health.

In one of their studies, Dr Grundy and Dr. Mattson developed three liquid diets. They were identical in all nutrients except fats. One contained saturated fat, one polyunsaturated fat, and one monounsaturated fat. Each of the twenty patients in the study followed each diet for four weeks. After the four-week periods, they were tested for changes in cholesterol levels.

Their total cholesterol levels rose on the saturated fat diet, while they were lowered on the polyunsaturated fat diet. However, the polyunsaturated diet lowered both their LDLs and their HDLs. The monounsaturated diet was equally effective in lowering total cholesterol levels but tended to target the LDLs for reduction and leave the HDLs alone. Further research confirmed these findings. Olive oil has also been linked to two other heart disease–related areas, diabetes and blood pressure.

In a 1988 study, Dr. Grundy and his associates studied patients with non-insulin-dependent diabetes, which usually begins after age forty and often affects individuals with a family history of diabetes. While these patients have been encouraged to eat a high-carbohydrate, low-fat diet, a growing body of research suggests that they may be better off replacing the saturated fat in their diet with unsaturated fat. In Dr. Grundy's experiment, half of the group ate a diet high in carbohydrates, such as fruits, vegetables and grains, but very low in fat, for twenty-eight days. On this diet, 60 percent of total calories came from carbohydrates and 25 percent came from fat. The other half of the group ate a diet that had 35 percent of its calories from carbohydrates and 50 percent from fat, in the form of olive oil. The diets were identical in terms of fibre and protein. The groups were switched after the initial twenty-eight days.

When the Grundy team examined the results, they found that when patients consumed high-fat diets, their blood sugar was lower and they required less insulin, proof that their diabetes was under better control. The high-fat diet also produced lower levels of triglycerides and LDLs but higher levels of HDLs. Dr Grundy's findings in this study reinforced those of earlier studies conducted by Dr. Gerald M. Reaven, a diabetes expert at Stanford University Medical Center.

Olive oil may also reduce high blood pressure, although more research needs to be done to bear out this finding.

Combined with the Mediterranean experience, the findings of American researchers suggest that adding monounsaturated fat to our diets while reducing polyunsaturated fats is a prudent step to be taken in the fight against heart disease. On the basis of centuries of use, monounsaturates appear to have the benefits of polyunsaturated fats without their drawbacks.

It would not be wise to totally eliminate polyunsaturates from the diet because a small amount of these fats are needed by the body as 'essential fatty acids.' However, we should seek polyunsaturates from natural food sources rather than relying on highly processed oils. Remember that olive oil includes 9 percent polyunsaturated fat.

The following breakdown has been suggested by Dr. Grundy and endorsed by Dr. Kenneth Cooper, the father of aerobics and acknowledged international leader in the field of disease prevention, in his book *Controlling Cholesterol* (Bantam, 1988).

* Keep saturated fats below 10 percent of total calories.

* Keep polyunsaturates between 5 and 10 percent of total calories.

* Keep monounsaturates between 10 and 15 percent of total calories.

Other medical and nutritional benefits of olive oil

In addition to its heart-protective role, olive oil has numerous other medical applications. The most exhaustive review to date of all aspects of the olive oil–health relationship was carried out by the Italian medical researchers Publio Fiola and Mirella Audisio. Summarizing scores of studies in their publication 'Olive Oil and Health' in 1986, Fiola and Audisio offer evidence that the olive's role in health and longevity in fact goes far beyond the reduction of coronary risk.

Some of the areas discussed in 'Olive Oil and Health' include:

* Digestion. Olive oil can also help the digestive system to function more efficiently. It is thought to reduce gastric acidity and to be effective in protecting against ulcers and gastritis. It also stimulates bile secretion and regulates the emptying of the gallbladder, reducing the risk of gallstones.

* Intestinal functions. Olive oil is the edible fat most easily absorbed by the intestines and regulates the passage of food through the intestines; 15–30 ml (1–2 tbsp) of olive oil has a positive effect as a laxative.

* Bone and brain development. Olive oil also promotes bone growth by fighting calcium loss and permits improved bone mineralisation in both children and adults due to its chemical composition. It is considered a good food choice for expectant and nursing mothers since it encourages normal brain development in the infant before and after birth. At the other end of the spectrum, olive oil may be helpful in preventing the wear and tear of age on brain functions and the aging of organs and tissues in general.

* Energy. Olive oil is an excellent source of energy since it metabolises readily thanks to its oleic oil content.

Other sources of monounsaturates

In addition to olive oil, there is one other oil currently on the market that has a high ratio of monounsaturates. This product is called rapeseed oil and is made from the rape plant that colours our fields such a vibrant yellow. Rapeseed oil is a staple of cooking in Canada, Japan, India and China. Although rapeseed oil and peanut oil both have large percentages of monounsaturates, olive oil has more. In addition, it has a much lower percentage of polyunsaturates than either rapeseed oil or peanut oil.

Olives, avocados and most nuts except walnuts and coconuts also contain a relatively high percentage of monounsaturates. While these foods can contribute to monounsaturate intake, they have a variety of limitations. Cured olives are high in sodium, nuts are high is saturated fats, and avocados are an unlikely choice for a daily staple. Although many animal products contain a relatively high percentage of monounsaturates, they also contain an excessive amount of saturated fat and cholesterol. 15 ml (1 tbsp) of olive oil contains 1.9 grams of saturated fat, 1.2 grams of polyunsaturated fat, 10.3 grams of monounsaturated fat, and 125 calories.

How to add olive oil to your diet

Adding olive oil to your diet will take planning and a change in some of your current eating habits. Since it is a fat, eating too much of it could cause you to gain weight. Consequently, you have to use it to replace other fats currently in your diet rather than simply adding fat calories in the form of olive oil.

How to Calculate Your Fat Calorie Consumption

1. Find out how many calories you should be eating each day to either maintain your weight if it is currently appropriate for your height and bone structure or to reduce it if you exceed your suggested weight range. Let's imagine, for example, that you will be eating 1,800 calories a day.

2. Estimate 30 percent of your total calories to find the maximum number of fat calories that you can eat every day. If you are eating 1,800 calories per day, you should eat no more than 540 calories (1800×.30) in the form of fats.

3. To determine how many calories of saturated fats you can eat each day, estimate 10 percent of your total calorie intake. If you are eating 1,800 calories a day, fewer that 180 (1800×.10) of these should be saturated fat.

4. To determine how many calories of polyunsaturated fat you can eat each day, estimate 5 percent of your total calorie intake. If you are eating 1,800 calories a day, approximately 90 (1800×.05) of these can be polyunsaturated fat.

5. To determine how many calories of monounsaturated fat you can eat each day, estimate 15 percent of your total calorie intake. If you are eating 1,800 calories a day, 270 (1800×.15) of these calories should be in the form of monounsaturated fat, ideally in the form of olive oil.

At the end of each of our recipes, you will find a list of the total fat, as well as the monounsaturated, polyunsaturated and saturated fat counts of the combined ingredients. Each of these counts will be listed in grams, kilojoules and calories for your convenience in computing your daily fat intake. Choose recipes that will provide the quantity of monounsaturated olive oil calories you need.

Fat contents are often presented on packaged foods in the form of grams. Since there are 9 calories in each gram of fat, you can compute the number of fat calories by multiplying the number of grams by 9.

SAMPLE DAILY FAT CONSUMPTION GUIDE				
Total Calories Consumed	**30% Fat**	**10% Sat**	**5% Poly**	**15% Mono**
3000	900	300	150	450
2000	600	200	100	300
1500	450	150	75	225

Including olive oil in a heart-healthy diet

While fats have a vital role to play in a cholesterol-lowering diet, they must be viewed as only one aspect of changing our overall approach to eating.

We need to focus on eating the correct number of calories, developing an exercise programme and avoiding processed foods that contain sugar, sodium, additives and preservatives. The ideal diet is one that is nutritionally sound and based on the Mediterranean tradition that includes less meat and high-fat dairy products and more fish, fresh fruit and vegetables, grains and olive oil.

Complex carbohydrates (fresh fruits, vegetables, breads and starches) should make up 50 to 60 percent of total calories; protein (fish, poultry, lean meat, dairy products, beans) should make up 10 to 20 percent. Fats (monounsaturates, polyunsaturates and saturates) should make up no more than 30 percent.

Shopping list of heart-healthy ingredients

* Buy olive oil, including mild, light-flavoured olive oil for cooking.

* Look out for 'lean choice' meat in butcher's shops, and supermarkets, labelling meat with stickers saying 'less than 10% fat'.

* Buy good quality minced beef steak with no more than 10 percent fat.

* Buy cholesterol-lowering oat bran to use as breadcrumbs.

* Choose low-salt vegetable stock cubes instead of beef or chicken stock cubes where possible.

* Buy fat-reduced cheeses, low-fat dairy spreads and skimmed milk dairy triangles.

* Buy low-fat cottage cheese. Whirl it in a blender or food processor and use as a substitute for soured cream or ricotta cheese. Try low-fat soft cheeses too.

* Buy large fresh eggs but limit egg yolk consumption to two a week in all foods.

* Order skimmed or semi-skimmed milk instead of whole milk. Buy skinned white meat poultry, which has a lower fat content than dark meat.

* Buy minced turkey.

* Buy natural brown rice since its bran layer has recently been found to lower cholesterol.

* Buy non-fat or low-fat plain yogurt.

* Choose half-fat alternatives instead of cream.

* Buy plenty of fish, fresh fruit and vegetables and pulses.

OLIVE OIL BASICS

The long, rich tradition of the olive tree, which Sophocles described as 'the tree that stands unequalled', is woven through the tapestry of human history.

Archaeologists have uncovered works of art that describe olive tree cultivation in the ancient world; many of the scenes they depict are still being acted out in the olive tree groves of the twentieth century.

Understanding how olives are grown and processed is a helpful tool in selecting olive oils and interpreting their labels. The steps in the process are harvesting, collection, grading, crushing and pressing. Each of these stages influences the final flavour of the oil.

The trees thrive mainly in the Mediterranean climatic zone, which produces 95 percent of the world's olive crop.

The lowering of the olive tree takes place between April and June. The flowers produce tiny berries the size of pinheads, which subsequently fill out with flesh and develop a hardened stone in the centre.

The olives contain no oil until they are pastel green in colour. At this point a chemical transformation begins to change sugars and organic acids into oil. This process continues until the olives have fully ripened and turned black. Olives that are harvested after they have turned black contain more oil than red-ripe olives, but their oil is more acidic.

Since olives are fragile they are frequently harvested by hand or with poles that have wooden or plastic comb heads. However, with mechanical assistance, the daily harvest per picker triples. The machines knock down 80 percent of the olives and the rest are knocked down by hand or with poles. Many experts feel that hand harvesting is essential to producing the finest quality oils since mechanical picking bruises the fruit and increases the acidity and tartness of the resulting oil.

In the collection phase, canvasses, nets or polyethylene covers are used beneath the trees to catch the falling olives and prevent them from touching the ground. Some resourceful growers even use open umbrellas placed upside down to catch the olives as they fall. Olives that touch the ground can become bruised and collect dirt, causing them to turn rancid.

The collected harvest is then poured into baskets and crates and picked over to clean out leaves, bits of twigs and unsound olives. Some producers allow leaves to remain to heighten the green colour of their oils. The olives are then graded according to their plumpness, stage of development, and quality either for oil or preserving. This process must be done by hand. It takes 5 kg (11 lb) of olives to obtain 1 litre ($1^3/_4$ pints) of oil. The average tree yields 2–4.3 litres ($4^1/_4$–$5^1/_4$ pints).

After cleaning, the olives are spread in thin layers on the floors of open-air sheds or packed in ice and stored for no longer than three days to prevent their fermenting. During this storage period, the water in their flesh evaporates, enabling them to more readily release a larger amount of oil. If olives are stored too long, they need to be chemically refined.

After the olives are removed from storage, they are washed, then crushed to a pulp by granite or stainless steel millstones.

The next step, pressing, extracts oil from the smooth, thick milled olive paste. The paste is then processed in one of two ways. Traditionally large hydraulic presses squeezed out the oil. Increasingly however, centrifugal force is used, spinning the paste at very high speed to separate the oil from it.

The oil produced in this way is called first cold pressed or virgin olive oil. In this state it has not been processed at all and it is the only vegetable oil that is fit for consumption without additional treatment. Regardless of the method used, the oil must be decanted, filtered and settled after pressing. If an oil is found to have less than 1 percent acidity and is considered perfect in flavour and aroma, it is called 'extra-virgin'. This oil must have a richness and depth of flavour that captures the essence of the olive itself. If it has an acid level of 1 to 3 percent, it is called 'virgin' olive oil and has a sharper taste.

The most widely available types of olive oil and their uses

The phenomenon of a product which is nutritious, tasty and versatile, but above all healthy, has been known to olive oil users in the Mediterranean for centuries. It is only in comparatively recent years that United Kingdom consumers have discovered the real benefits of using olive oil.

This book aims to help consumers make the most of olive oil with a nutritious and healthy selection of recipes. It also aims to reduce the mystery surrounding olive oil and to explain the various types of olive oil and their uses.

Extra Virgin Olive Oil

To receive the accolade 'extra' virgin olive oil, this completely natural product of the first pressing of the olives must achieve an absolutely perfect colour and flavour and have an acidity of less than 1 percent. Of course there are ordinary virgin oils on the market, but these have a higher acidity and are, therefore, not marketed under the premium FILIPPO BERIO label.

FILIPPO BERIO offer three styles of extra-virgin olive oil: the normal high-quality Extra-Virgin Olive Oil; the premium quality 'Special Selection' Extra-Virgin Olive Oil; the highly prized 'Farmhouse Unfiltered' Extra-Virgin Olive Oil.

The full aroma and flavour of extra-virgin olive oil adds authenticity to a wide variety of Mediterranean cuisine, including pizza and pasta dishes, and is also ideal for dressing salads.

Pure Olive Oil

FILIPPO BERIO's reputation for quality is highlighted in the content of virgin olive oil blended with refined oil to produce Pure Olive Oil. Economies effected by using less virgin olive oil lead to cheaper, inferior products and should be avoided.

Pure Olive Oil can fulfil all of the functions of extra-virgin olive oil in recipes where a less pronounced flavour is required. It may also be used as a base for home-made salad dressings, mayonnaise and marinades.

Light Olive Oil

This specially refined oil is an innovation which, with its mild flavour and light texture, has firmly established olive oil as an everyday cooking oil.

FILIPPO BERIO Mild & Light Olive Oil retains all the health benefits, whilst its high smokepoint and slower breakdown compared to other oils, makes it ideal for either deep or shallow frying, stir-frying and baking.

Cooking with olive oil

Olive oils differ in quality, smoke point, colour, flavour and aroma. Each type of olive oil has its own purpose. Genuine extra-virgin oil has the richest, deepest flavour and captures the essence of the olive itself, but isn't appropriate for every dish. Since cooking reduces the flavour of extra-virgin oil, it's a waste of money to use it in baking, sauces or recipes in which other ingredients might overpower its taste. Save it for salads and other cold dishes or trickle it over hot dishes just before serving so the rich flavour can be fully enjoyed. Use it in dishes such as pasta with oil and garlic, where is is the featured ingredient. Use lesser quality oils in dishes where the flavour will be dominated by the other ingredients. Their lighter nature allows the flavours of the food to come through, and they are usually preferred for sautéeing and frying.

Cooking oils should not be allowed to smoke since the chemical structure of fats and oils is changed when heated beyond the smoking point. Olive oil, unlike seed oils, remains stable at relatively high temperatures because of its antioxidant and high oleic acid content. Pure olive oils have smoking points ranging from 207–242°C (406–468°F).

Olive oil, like wine, also offers a wide range of flavours, colours and aromas that vary with the nature of the soil and climate where the olives were cultivated and the type of olive used. In fact, olive oil is the only cooking and salad oil that offers a variety of natural flavours.

Flavours can vary from bland to peppery and can be described as mild (delicate, light and almost buttery tasting), semi-fruity (stronger with more olive taste), fruity (oil with a strong olive flavour), pizzico (oil with a peppery accent), rustic (hearty oil), and sweet.

Colours can range from delicate straw hues to emerald green. While dark, intense colour may signal a fruity flavour and lighter colours may indicate a nuttier flavour, this is not always the case since oils are often blends of several varieties of olives. Like wines, olive oils have vintages caused by changes in growing conditions that affect colour and flavour. In fact, you might buy two very green oils and discover that one is intensely peppery and the other light and fruity.

Since no two olive oils are alike they should be chosen as you would choose wine, by personal taste preference and budget considerations. Beware of oils that have a thick, greasy appearance or those that are thin, pallid and watery. Also avoid those that have been stored in the sun or have a copper tint.

Choosing olive oils

To begin with, you'll want to buy one costlier genuine extra-virgin oil and one lesser quality oil. Select cold-pressed oils whenever possible. Although this phrase suggests that the oil has been removed without heat and is therefore more nutritionally sound, some heat may have actually been used in the extraction process. The important word is 'pressed' since it indicates that oil has been produced by an expellor method.

The best way to taste olive oil is by dipping crusty bread or lightly steamed vegetables into it or sipping it from a spoon or a tiny cup. If you are tasting several oils at the same time, use mineral water, soda water or white wine to cleanse the palate between tastings. A fatty sensation in the throat or a highly acidic taste are both negative signs.

Storing olive oil

Light is harmful to olive oil, so it should be stored in a cool, dark place. Keep it away from dampness and do not expose it to heat, light or air for any length of time. You can pour olive oil into a green glass wine bottle with a cork to prevent spoilage from ultra-violet rays. It can also be stored in stainless steel or glazed ceramic.

Avoid buying olive oil in plastic containers because some of the compounds used in the manufacture of the plastic may be absorbed by the oil. If you have to buy oil packaged in plastic, transfer it to a glass or stainless steel container after you open it since contact with oxygen can trigger the chemical reaction.

Olive oil has less of a tendency to turn rancid than most other oils due to its low iodine value. Olive oil does not improve with age. If stored correctly, fine olive oils can be kept for at least a year. Oils are most flavourful for the first two months and begin to lose their tangy olive taste after twelve months.

If you are worried about having the oil spoil, you can store it in the refrigerator. The flavour will remain intact, but the oil will get cloudy. You can use the cloudy oil or wait until it returns to room temperature. You can speed up the process by placing the bottle under warm tap water for a few minutes. Another alternative is to keep a small amount of oil on your kitchen shelf while storing the larger bottle in the refrigerator.

Twenty easy ways to add olive oil to your diet

1.   Keep a cruet of olive oil on your dining table and sprinkle it on salads, soups, stews and pasta.

2.   Toss hot or cold vegetables with 30 ml (2 tbsp) olive oil, freshly ground black pepper and a squeeze of fresh lemon juice.

3.   Toss salad greens with olive oil, then with lemon juice or vinegar. Tossing with oil first will keep the greens from wilting.

4.   Dip raw vegetables in a dipping sauce made with olive oil and freshly ground black pepper.

5.   Stir-fry vegetables with 30 ml (2 tbsp) olive oil, 2 crushed garlic cloves and a sprinkling of fresh herbs.

6.   Make vegetable sauces by sautéeing finely diced vegetables in olive oil. Add wine and stock and simmer,

7.   Use olive oil to replace the rich taste of meat or meat broth in your favourite soup and stew recipes.

8.   Reduce the saturated fat in butter sauces by substituting a stock thickened with olive oil. Boil a fish or chicken stock and thicken it by adding a steady stream of olive oil. Add additional stock as needed and simmer. Season by adding 30–45 ml (2–3 tbsp) wine.

9.   Bake cubes of winter vegetables, such as fresh swede or parsnip, in olive oil, parsley and garlic.

10.   Rub potatoes with olive oil before baking for added crispness. Serve with more olive oil, herbs and pepper.

11.   Add 15 ml (1 tbsp) olive oil to water when boiling pasta to prevent the pasta from sticking to the pot. Toss cooked pasta with 15 ml (1 tbsp) olive oil immediately after draining.

12.   To add flavour, first brown meat in olive oil when braising it before cooking in liquid.

13.   When grilling or roasting meats or poultry, brush with olive oil to seal in the natural juices.

14.   Pan-grill meat, poultry or fish in an uncovered frying pan lightly coated with olive oil.

15.   Prepare drop-scone and waffle batter using light-flavoured olive oil. Also use olive oil to grease the griddle.

16. Substitute light-flavoured olive oil for other liquid oils in baking recipes. It is particularly compatible with fruit cakes and fruit muffins.

17. Pop corn in olive oil and drizzle some extra oil over the top of the popped corn.

18. Use olive oil as a spread for bread and rolls instead of butter or margarine. When dining out, ask your waitress for a cruet of olive oil for this purpose.

19. Make croûtons by sprinkling cubes of French bread with olive oil and black pepper. Bake at 200°C (400°F) mark 6 until toasted.

20. Sauté breadcrumbs with olive oil and paprika until golden brown. Add to steamed vegetables and salads.

THE 'FILIPPO BERIO' STORY

FILIPPO BERIO is one of the oldest and most famous names in Italian olive oil. The brand first appeared around 1850 and, during the second half of the nineteenth century, won many gold medals at trade fairs in Europe and North America. Lucca, an ancient walled city in Tuscany, has for centuries been considered the home of the world's finest olive oil. Lucca is also the home of the Fontana family, which has owned the FILIPPO BERIO brand for four generations.

In the 1990s, sophisticated modern equipment is used in the production of FILIPPO BERIO olive oil, and the strictest quality control is carried out in computerised laboratories. From Lucca, FILIPPO BERIO olive oil is exported throughout the world. The USA is by far the largest market for the brand, and FILIPPO BERIO has been present on the American market for more than a century. FILIPPO BERIO can be found as far away as Japan and Australia, but its second largest market is Great Britain, where it has been brand leader since 1985. The distinctive gold labelling of FILIPPO BERIO olive oil is now a familiar sight in food stores throughout Britain. British consumers have been quick to appreciate that these high quality olive oils will enhance the flavour of their food, and form part of a balanced, healthy diet.

If you would like further product or health information concerning FILIPPO BERIO olive oils, please write to:

> FILIPPO BERIO INFORMATION SERVICE
> RAANS ROAD
> AMERSHAM
> BUCKS HP6 6JJ

USING THE RECIPES

Nutrient analysis

Following each recipe, you will find a nutritional analysis that includes:

a. Calories (cal) per serving
b. Grams (gm) of protein
c. Grams of carbohydrate
d. Grams of dietary fibre
e. Milligrams (mg) of cholesterol
f. Total fat (in grams and calories)
g. Saturated (sat) fat (in grams and calories)
h. Polyunsaturated (poly) fat (in grams and calories)
i. Monounsaturated (mono) fat (in grams and calories)

The analyses of meat, poultry and seafood ingredients are based on a single portion serving of meat, poultry or seafood of 100 g (4 oz). When a choice of ingredients is suggested, we have based our analysis on the first ingredient listed.

Total fat calories are not always equal to the total of saturated, polyunsaturated and monounsaturated fat calories in the nutrition counts due to gaps in currently available data on food values.

Due to inevitable variations in the ingredients you may select, nutritional analyses should be considered approximate.

Super-quick recipes

Our Q symbol above the preparation time given for a recipe indicates a combined preparation and cooking time of 35 minutes or less.

STARTERS & SNACKS

Aubergine Caviar

This dish is often called 'poor man's caviar' in southern France. Since real caviar is not only expensive but high in cholesterol, this delicious substitute is a bargain in more ways than one. Serve it at room temperature or chilled as a spread with savoury biscuits or toast.

2 aubergines, about 450 g (1 lb)
30 ml (2 tbsp) finely chopped spring onions
1 clove garlic, crushed
10 ml (2 tsp) lemon juice
2.5 ml (¹/₂ tsp) dried basil
60 ml (4 tbsp) extra-virgin olive oil
1.25 ml (¹/₄ tsp) black pepper

1. Preheat oven to 200°C (400°F) mark 6. Cut aubergines in half lengthways and place on a baking sheet with their cut-sides facing down. Bake for 20 minutes or until they are tender.

2. Take aubergines out of oven and remove the pulp from the skin. Purée pulp in a blender. Spoon into medium bowl.

3. Combine aubergine pulp with remaining ingredients. Serve at room temperature or chill for 1 hour.

Variation
Omit the basil. Add 1.25 ml (¹/₄ tsp) crushed dried chillies for a spicier spread.

serves 4

Q

preparation time

15 minutes

cooking time

20 minutes

nutrient analysis

Calories per serving: 185
Protein: 2 gm
Carbohydrates: 16 gm
Dietary fibre: 6.4 gm
Cholesterol: 0 mg
Total fat: 14 gm (126 cal)
Sat fat: 2 gm (18 cal)
Poly fat: 1.4 gm (12.6 cal)
Mono fat: 10 gm (90 cal)

Raw Vegetables with Tangy Cheese Dip

serves 4

Q

preparation time

10 minutes

nutrient analysis

Calories per serving: 147
Protein: 4.5 gm
Carbohydrates: 1.6 gm
Dietary fibre: 0.05 gm
Cholesterol: 1.6 mg
Total fat: 13.9 gm (125 cal)
Sat fat: 2.1 gm (19 cal)
Poly fat: 1.2 gm (10 cal)
Mono fat: 10 gm (90 cal)

Prepare a tray of vegetables such as steamed asparagus spears, blanched broccoli and cauliflower florets, spring onions, carrot and celery sticks, turnip wedges, green pepper strips, mushrooms, mangetout, radishes, cucumber and courgette chunks, baby tomatoes and green beans. Serve with an assortment of oatcakes, whole grain crackers or pita bread wedges and a bowl of this delicious Tangy Cheese Dip.

150 ml (¼ pint) low-fat cottage cheese
10 ml (2 tsp) red wine vinegar
60 ml (4 tbsp) olive oil
5 ml (1 tsp) grated orange rind
1 clove garlic, crushed
15 ml (1 tbsp) chopped spring onions
1.25 ml (¼ tsp) black pepper

Process all ingredients at medium speed in a blender or food processor until thoroughly blended. Use a rubber spatula to push down mixture to blend well.

Variations
★ Omit orange rind and red wine vinegar. Add 15 ml (1 tbsp) caraway seed, 7.5 ml (1½ tsp) mild paprika, 15 ml (1 tbsp) chopped celery, 30 ml (2 tbsp) chopped radish.
★ Omit red wine vinegar and orange rind. Add 5 ml (1 tsp) Dijon mustard, 2.5 ml (½ tsp) dried tarragon, 15 ml (1 tbsp) chopped fresh parsley, 2.5 ml (½ tsp) anchovy paste.
★ Add 2.5 ml (½ tsp) curry powder.
★ Omit orange rind. Add 25 g (1 oz) chopped mushrooms and 25 ml (1½ tbsp) fresh dill.
★ Omit orange rind and spring onions. Add 15 ml (1 tbsp) finely chopped fresh mint, 15 ml (1 tbsp) chopped fresh dill, and 15 ml (1 tbsp) snipped fresh chives.
★ Omit orange rind. Add 30 ml (2 tbsp) chopped cucumber, 30 ml (2 tbsp) chopped radish, 15 ml (1 tbsp) chopped green pepper, 15 ml (1 tbsp) chopped fresh parsley, 15 ml (1 tbsp) chopped fresh dill.
★ Add 40 g (1½ oz) chopped black olives.
★ Add 25 g (1 oz) chopped blanched almonds.
★ Omit red wine vinegar and orange rind. Add 75 g (3 oz)

chopped canned clams, drained; 15 ml (1 tbsp) chopped fresh parsley, 30 ml (2 tbsp) lemon juice.
* Add crushed dried chillies to taste.
* Omit orange rind. Add 6 cooked, chopped prawns.
* Add 30 ml (2 tbsp) chopped cucumber.
* Omit orange rind. Add ¹/₂ ripe avocado, peeled, seeded, and chopped; 15 ml (1 tbsp) fresh dill and 15 ml (1 tbsp) snipped fresh chives.

Mushrooms with Oil and Lemon

Select button mushrooms with tight white caps. This dish should be served warm or at room temperature with the oil it was cooked in.

450 g (1 lb) button mushrooms, wiped
125 ml (4 fl oz) extra-virgin olive oil
1 clove garlic, cut in half
1.25 ml (¹/₄ tsp) salt
15 ml (1 tbsp) lemon juice
15 ml (1 tbsp) chopped fresh parsley

1. Trim mushroom stems.
2. Heat oil in a frying pan over moderate heat, and sauté garlic clove until it turns light brown. With a slotted spoon, remove garlic and discard.
3. Add mushrooms to oil and sauté for 1 minute. Add salt. Sauté mushrooms, stirring constantly, for 4 additional minutes.
4. Add lemon juice and parsley to pan and stir to combine with mushrooms.
5. Remove from heat and serve.

Variation
Mexican Mushroom Starter: Add pinch of crushed dried chillies and 2.5 ml (¹/₂ tsp) dried oregano.

serves 6

Q

preparation time

10 minutes

cooking time

8 minutes

nutrient analysis

Calories per serving: 180
Protein: 1.6 gm
Carbohydrates: 4 gm
Dietary fibre: 1.4 gm
Cholesterol: 0 mg
Total fat: 18 gm (164 cal)
Sat fat: 2.6 gm (23 cal)
Poly fat: 1.7 gm (15 cal)
Mono fat: 13 gm (119 cal)

serves 4

preparation time

15 minutes + 30 minutes of
marinating

cooking time

20 minutes

nutrient analysis

Calories per serving: 475
Protein: 37 gm
Carbohydrates: 10 gm
Dietary fibre: 0 gm
Cholesterol: 94 mg
Total fat: 32 gm (284 cal)
Sat fat: 5 gm (46 cal)
Poly fat: 3.2 gm (29 cal)
Mono fat: 21 gm (191 cal)

Garlic Chicken Bites

These crispy chicken nuggets are seasoned with garlic,
cayenne and black pepper. Serve warm and dip in a honey-
mustard sauce or the Chilli Barbecue Sauce (p. 147).

2 boneless chicken breasts (450 g/1 lb), skinned and cut into
    bite-sized strips
125 ml (4 fl oz) extra-virgin olive oil
4 cloves garlic, crushed
1.25 ml (¼ tsp) black pepper
25 g (1 oz) fresh breadcrumbs (or oat bran)
1.25 ml (¼ tsp) cayenne pepper

1.   Marinate chicken strips in olive oil, garlic and pepper
for 30 minutes. Drain off excess marinade. Preheat oven to
240°C (475°F) mark 9.
2.   Mix breadcrumbs with cayenne. Dip both sides of
chicken strips in mixture.
3.   Arrange strips in one layer on a baking sheet. Bake
for 15 minutes. Turn and bake 5 minutes more until
browned.

Walnut-Orange Chicken Bites

Marinate the chicken in orange juice and sherry overnight
and cook it just before serving. Serve on a bed of lettuce.

30 ml (2 tbsp) sherry
60 ml (4 tbsp) orange juice
pared rind of ½ orange, cut into thin strips
60 ml (4 tbsp) olive oil
1.25 ml (¼ tsp) black pepper
2 boneless chicken breasts (450 g/1 lb), skinned and cut into
    2.5-cm (1-inch) pieces
50 g (2 oz) chopped walnuts

serves 4

preparation time

10 minutes + overnight
marinating time

cooking time

10 minutes

nutrient analysis

Calories per serving: 384
Protein: 38 gm
Carbohydrates: 3 gm
Dietary fibre: 0.6 gm
Cholesterol: 96 mg
Total fat: 23 gm (207 cal)
Sat fat: 3.4 gm (30 cal)
Poly fat: 5.7 gm (51 cal)
Mono fat: 12.6 gm (113 cal)

1.   Combine the sherry, orange juice, orange rind, 30 ml
(2 tbsp) of the oil, and pepper in a glass bowl.
2.   Add the chicken, cover and marinate overnight.
3.   Drain chicken on absorbent kitchen paper. Save the
orange rind and discard the marinade.
4.   Heat remaining olive oil in a frying pan and sauté
chicken pieces, stirring constantly, for 10 minutes until
tender. Stir in orange rind and walnuts immediately before
removing from frying pan.

Lady Meatballs

These Syrian meatballs, also called *Kadin Budu*, are made with rice, Parmesan cheese and dill. Serve very hot on cocktail sticks. They can be made ahead and reheated when ready to serve.

50 g (2 oz) cooked rice
450 g (1 lb) lean turkey mince (or lamb or minced beef)
50 g (2 oz) grated onion
30 ml (2 tbsp) chopped fresh parsley
40 g (1¹/₂ oz) grated Parmesan cheese
75 ml (5 tbsp) olive oil
2 egg whites, beaten
30 ml (2 tbsp) chopped fresh dill (or 10 ml (2 tsp) dried dill)
1.25 ml (¹/₄ tsp) black pepper
50g (2 oz) plain flour (or 25 g (1 oz) flour and 25 g (1 oz) oat bran)

1. Combine rice, meat, onion, parsley, cheese, 30 ml (2 tbsp) of the olive oil, egg whites, dill and pepper in a bowl.

2. Knead well and form into 20 ovals.

3. Roll ovals in flour or flour and bran mixture.

4. Heat remaining oil over moderate heat in a large frying pan. Fry ovals for about 5 minutes until brown on one side. Turn carefully and fry other side for 3 minutes or until brown. Remove and drain on absorbent kitchen paper.

5. Keep in a covered casserole in a warm oven until ready to serve. If refrigerating to serve later, reheat in a covered casserole at 160°C (325°F) mark 3 for 20 minutes until warmed through.

makes 20 (4 servings)

preparation time

20 minutes (not including cooking rice)

cooking time

10 minutes

nutrient analysis

Calories per serving: 455
Protein: 43 gm
Carbohydrates: 19 gm
Dietary fibre: 1.2 gm
Cholesterol: 104 mg
Total fat: 22 gm (198 cal)
Sat fat: 5.1 gm (45 cal)
Poly fat: 1.7 gm (15 cal)
Mono fat: 14 gm (126 cal)

Ecuadorian Prawn Seviche

serves 8

preparation time

*30 minutes + overnight
marinating time*

cooking time

5 minutes

nutrient analysis

*Calories per serving: 228
Protein: 13 gm
Carbohydrates: 13 gm
Dietary fibre: 1 gm
Cholesterol: 100 mg
Total fat: 14 gm (128 cal)
Sat fat: 2 gm (18 cal)
Poly fat: 1.4 gm (12 cal)
Mono fat: 10 gm (90 cal)*

Seviche, a multi-flavoured Mexican speciality, is a fresh fish or shellfish starter that is 'cooked' in freshly squeezed fruit juices. This Ecuadorian version of seviche uses a medley of fruit juices and lightly-steamed prawns and can be served like a prawn cocktail in individual lettuce-lined goblets. It is essential to use prawns that are absolutely fresh.

*450 g (1 lb) fresh medium or large prawns, peeled and
   deveined
60 ml (4 tbsp) water
2.5 ml (¹/₂ tsp) salt
15 ml (1 tbsp) black pepper
250 ml (8 fl oz) fresh fruit juice (combination of lemon,
   lime and orange)
1 large red onion, very thinly sliced
2 large ripe tomatoes, very thinly sliced
1 clove garlic, crushed
60 ml (4 tbsp) extra-virgin olive oil
5 ml (1 tsp) horseradish sauce
250 ml (8 fl oz) chilli sauce
30 ml (2 tbsp) chopped fresh parsley
30 ml (2 tbsp) chopped fresh coriander*

1.   Rinse prawns in running water, put in a medium saucepan and add 60 ml (4 tbsp) of water. Cover pan and simmer over low heat until water boils, then remove from heat immediately.

2.   Allow to stand for 3 or 4 minutes, then remove prawns from water with a slotted spoon. Strain prawn water from pan and refrigerate for use the following day when you assemble the seviche.

3.   Place the prawns in a glass bowl with 1.25 ml (¹/₄ tsp) of the salt, 2.5 ml (¹/₂ tsp) of the pepper, and half the fruit juice. Stir, cover, and leave to marinate in the refrigerator overnight.

4.   In a second glass bowl, combine sliced onion and tomatoes. Add garlic, olive oil, and remaining salt, pepper and fruit juice. Cover bowl and marinate overnight.

5.   Before serving, combine prawn and vegetable mixtures. Stir in horseradish sauce, chilli sauce, parsley, coriander and water reserved from steaming prawns. Mix well and serve. Serve with additional chilli sauce.

Crab Salad Cocktail

Olive oil gives a new dimension to this favourite delicacy from Maryland, USA. Serve the crab mixture mounded into empty crab shells or use it as a stuffing for hollowed-out baby tomatoes.

450 g (1 lb) cooked crabmeat
45 ml (3 tbsp) finely chopped fresh parsley
60 ml (4 tbsp) extra-virgin olive oil
juice of 1 large lemon
1.25 ml (¹/₄ tsp) white pepper

1. Shred the crabmeat in a bowl with a fork and combine with parsley.
2. Add oil and lemon juice. Sprinkle with white pepper. Stuff shells or tomatoes and chill thoroughly before serving.

serves 4

Q

preparation time

10 minutes

nutrient analysis

Calories per serving: 237
Protein: 20 gm
Carbohydrates: 2.4 gm
Dietary fibre: 0.2 gm
Cholesterol: 113 mg
Total fat: 16.2 gm (146 cal)
Sat fat: 2.4 gm (21 cal)
Poly fat: 2.8 gm (25 cal)
Mono fat: 10.4 gm (94 cal)

Bruschetta

Bruschetta is the Italian ancestor of garlic bread. It can be prepared with or without the tomato slices. Serve on a platter with slices of mozzarella cheese and green Italian olives.

8×2.5-cm (¹/₂-inch) thick slices French or Italian bread
2 cloves garlic, cut in half
60 ml (4 tbsp) olive oil
2 medium ripe tomatoes, thinly sliced
2.5 ml (¹/₂ tsp) black pepper

1. Toast bread under a hot grill until lightly browned on both sides.
2. Rub top of bread with garlic. Return slices to grill pan.
3. Sprinkle olive oil over toast slices. Top with tomato slices and pepper.
4. Grill close to heat for 1 minute and serve at once.

Variation
Crush garlic and spread on bread.

serves 4

Q

preparation time

10 minutes

cooking time

5 minutes

nutrient analysis

Calories per serving: 303
Protein: 6.6 gm
Carbohydrates: 37 gm
Dietary fibre: 1.7 gm
Cholesterol: 0 mg
Total fat: 13.6 gm (122 cal)
Sat fat: 1.9 gm (17 cal)
Poly fat: 1.2 gm (10 cal)
Mono fat: 10 gm (90 cal)

Tuna Caponata

serves 6

preparation time

30 minutes

cooking time

20 minutes

nutrient analysis

Calories per serving: 227
Protein: 11.9 gm
Carbohydrates: 14 gm
Dietary fibre: 4.2 gm
Cholesterol: 12.4 mg
Total fat: 15.4 gm (139 cal)
Sat fat: 2 gm (19 cal)
Poly fat: 1.7 gm (15 cal)

Traditionally, caponata is served at room temperature; however, it can also be served hot or chilled. You can present it as an hors d'oeuvre with French bread or as a side dish with grilled meat or fish.

90 ml (6 tbsp) extra-virgin olive oil
1 medium aubergine (about 450 g (1 lb)), peeled and cut into 2 cm (³/₄ inch) slices
1.25 ml (¹/₄ tsp) black pepper
100 g (4 oz) celery, chopped
2 medium onions, chopped
1 medium red pepper, seeded and cut into 2 cm (³/₄ inch) chunks
2 courgettes, cut in half lengthways, then into 2.5-cm (¹/₂-inch) slices.
250 g (9 oz) chopped ripe tomatoes (or 250 g (9 oz) drained chopped canned tomatoes)
60 ml (4 tbsp) red wine vinegar
2.5 ml (¹/₂ tsp) fresh thyme (or 1.25 ml (¹/₄ tsp) dried thyme)
1.25 ml (¹/₄ tsp) ground cloves
5 ml (1 tsp) sugar
8 green olives, rinsed in cold water, stoned and chopped
198 g (7 oz) can tuna (preferably yellow-fin), packed in water, drained and mixed with 15 ml (1 tbsp) olive oil

1. Heat 60 ml (4 tbsp) of the olive oil in a large frying pan. Add aubergine and season with pepper. Cook over high heat until aubergine is lightly browned, about 8 minutes. Remove with slotted spoon and set aside in a large bowl.

2. Add 2 more tablespoons of olive oil to pan and sauté celery for 5 minutes over moderate heat. Add onions and cook for 2 minutes more or until onions are soft. Add red pepper and courgettes to pan and sauté for 4 minutes more.

3. Add tomatoes, cover, and cook over moderate heat for 6 minutes. Return aubergine to pan, stir and simmer over low heat for 5 minutes.

4. In a small saucepan, heat vinegar, thyme, cloves, sugar and olives for 30 seconds.

5. Add vinegar mixture to pan. Cover and simmer for 5 more minutes.

6. Flake the tuna and sprinkle on top of the caponata immediately before serving.

SOUPS

Bean Soups

Beans are low in fat and cholesterol-free. In addition, research has proved their effectiveness in lowering harmful low-density lipoproteins (LDLs) in blood cholesterol.

Sort through beans before cooking them, removing any that are discoloured and any pebbles or other particles that may be present.

There are two ways to soak dried beans to prepare them for cooking.

1. Rinse and soak the beans overnight in enough water to cover the beans plus 5 cm (2 inches) extra to compensate for absorption. When drained the next morning, they're ready to use.
2. The quicker method is to cover the beans with water in a large pan and bring to the boil for 2 minutes. Remove from the heat and soak for 1 hour. After draining and rinsing, they're ready to use.

Lentils don't need to be soaked. Other varieties of small beans such as green peas may also indicate on their packages that soaking isn't necessary.

Bean-Leek Soup

serves 4

preparation time

20 minutes

cooking time

40 minutes

nutrient analysis

Calories per serving: 393
Protein: 15 gm
Carbohydrates: 38 gm
Dietary fibre: 9.6 gm
Cholesterol: 1.0 mg
Total fat: 21 gm (187 cal)
Sat fat: 3.1 gm (28 cal)
Poly fat: 2.1 gm (19 cal)
Mono fat: 13.9 gm (125 cal)

This easy-to-prepare soup combines mild, sweet leeks with deep-red kidney beans and round, golden chick-peas, and then adds fresh green beans for good measure. Serve topped with fresh parsley and croûtons.

75 ml (5 tbsp) olive oil
2 leeks, trimmed and chopped
2 sticks of celery, chopped
2 cloves garlic, crushed
1 litre (1³/₄ pints) water
2 low-salt vegetable stock cubes, crumbled
5 ml (1 tsp) dried thyme
5 ml (1 tsp) dried marjoram
1 bay leaf
1.25 ml (¹/₄ tsp) black pepper
250 g (9 oz) cooked kidney beans
250 g (9 oz) cooked chick-peas
450 g (1 lb) fresh green beans, topped, tailed and cut into
    2.5 cm (1 inch) pieces

1.   Heat olive oil in a large, heavy soup pan over moderate heat and sauté leeks, celery and garlic until tender.
2.   Add water, stock cubes, thyme, marjoram, bay leaf, pepper, kidney beans and chick-peas. Bring ingredients to the boil, then lower heat to simmer for 25 minutes.
3.   Add green beans and simmer for 10 minutes more.

Split Pea Soup

Split peas are available in green and yellow, the yellow peas having a less pronounced flavour, but both are good. Top soup with croutons or add 25 g (1 oz) warm, cooked rice in the bottom of each soup bowl. Serve with rye bread and Shredded Carrot-Turnip Slaw. (p. 52).

60 ml (4 tbsp) olive oil
2 medium onions, chopped
2 cloves garlic, chopped
250 g (8 oz) dried split peas, sorted and rinsed
1.5 litres (2¾ pints) water
75 g (3 oz) carrots, sliced
1 stick of celery, chopped
1 bay leaf
1.25 ml (¼ tsp) black pepper

1. Heat olive oil in a large, heavy soup pan over moderate heat and sauté onion and garlic for 5 minutes or until softened.
2. Stir in split peas, water, carrots, celery, bay leaf and black pepper.
3. Reduce heat and simmer for 2 hours, stirring frequently.

serves 6

preparation time
20 minutes

cooking time
2 hours

nutrient analysis
Calories per serving: 173
Protein: 5.9 gm
Carbohydrates: 18 gm
Dietary fibre: 0.9 gm
Cholesterol: 0 mg
Total fat: 9.5 gm (86 cal)
Sat fat: 1.3 gm (12 cal)
Poly fat: 0.8 gm (7 cal)
Mono fat: 7 gm (60 cal)

Lima Bean Soup

The special richness of olive oil replaces the salty meats often used to provide flavour in bean soups in this hearty wintertime Tuscan favourite. Additional olive oil can be added at the table.

serves 4

---

preparation time

30 minutes + bean soaking time (overnight)

---

cooking time

1 hour and 15 minutes

---

nutrient analysis

Calories per serving: 365
Protein: 13 gm
Carbohydrates: 30 gm
Dietary fibre: 4.8 gm
Cholesterol: 1.0 mg
Total fat: 22 gm (198 cal)
Sat fat: 3.4 gm (30 cal)
Poly fat: 2.2 gm (20 cal)
Mono fat: 15.6 gm (140 cal)

450 g (1 lb) dried lima beans, sorted and rinsed
1 litre (1³/₄ pints) water
2 low-salt vegetable stock cubes, crumbled
2 bay leaves
10 ml (2 tsp) dried oregano
90 ml (6 tbsp) olive oil
45 ml (3 tbsp) chopped fresh parsley
4 cloves garlic, crushed
75 ml (5 tbsp) lemon juice

1.   Place beans in a large bowl, cover with 5 cm (2 inches) extra water, and soak overnight.

2.   Drain beans and pour into a large, heavy soup pan. Add water, stock cubes, bay leaves, oregano and olive oil. Bring to the boil over high heat, then reduce heat to low, cover and simmer for 1 hour.

3.   Purée half the beans and half the liquid in a blender or food processor. Pour the purée back into the soup pan containing the remaining beans and liquid.

4.   Add the parsley, garlic and lemon juice. Simmer for 15 minutes.

Soup with Pistou Garnish

A fragrant purée of basil, garlic and olive oil is added to this hearty, nourishing vegetable, bean and pasta soup just before serving. Serve with Herb Bread (p. 166) and spread with Pine Nut Parmesan Pesto (p. 158).

Soup

50 g (2 oz) chopped celery
50 g (2 oz) chopped onion
350 g (12 oz) fresh green beans, topped, tailed and cut into
    2.5-cm (1-inch) pieces or 275 g (10 oz) sliced frozen
    green beans
100 g (4 oz) sliced carrots
3 medium potatoes, peeled and cut into 2.5-cm (1-inch)
    cubes
2 medium courgettes, sliced
2 medium tomatoes, roughly chopped
2 bay leaves
1.25 ml (¹/₄ tsp) black pepper
75 g (3 oz) elbow macaroni
175 g (6 oz) cooked drained red kidney beans

Pistou

3 cloves garlic, crushed
25 g (1 oz) fresh basil leaves
60 ml (4 tbsp) olive oil

Topping

50 g (2 oz) grated Parmesan cheese

1. Place celery, onion, beans, carrots, potatoes, courgettes, tomatoes, bay leaves and black pepper in a large, heavy soup pan. Add enough water to cover plus 5 cm (2 inches). Bring to the boil over high heat, then reduce heat to low and simmer for 20 minutes or until vegetables are crisp-tender.

2. Add macaroni and kidney beans. Raise heat to high and quickly bring to the boil. Reduce heat to moderate and cook for 15 minutes more.

3. Prepare pistou by blending garlic, basil and olive oil in blender or food processor until smooth, scraping down the sides of the container as needed.

4. Spoon equal portions of the pistou into 4 soup bowls. Add soup to bowls and garnish with Parmesan cheese.

serves 4

preparation time
30 minutes

cooking time
40 minutes

nutrient analysis

Calories per serving: 450
Protein: 16 gm
Carbohydrates: 59 gm
Dietary fibre: 9.8 gm
Cholesterol: 10 mg
Total fat: 19 gm (171 cal)
Sat fat: 4.5 gm (40 cal)
Poly fat: 1.6 gm (14 cal)
Mono fat: 11 gm (100 cal)

Minestrone with Pesto

serves 4

Q

preparation time

15 minutes

cooking time

22 minutes

nutrient analysis

Calories per serving: 228
Protein: 1.8 gm
Carbohydrates: 11 gm
Dietary fibre: 2.6 gm
Cholesterol: 0 mg
Total fat: 20.6 gm (186 cal)
Sat fat: 2.9 gm (26 cal)
Poly fat: 1.9 gm (17 cal)
Mono fat: 15 gm (134 cal)

Serve this quick version of minestrone with Oregano Parsley Pesto (p. 158) and grated Parmesan cheese.

60 ml (4 tbsp) mild, light-flavoured olive oil
50 g (2 oz) chopped onion
75 g (3 oz) chopped fresh or canned tomatoes
75 g (3 oz) chopped carrots
75 g (3 oz) chopped green cabbage
150 g (5 oz) chopped courgettes
1 litre (1³/₄ pints) water
3 spring onions, chopped
75 g (3 oz) diced, peeled potatoes
50 g (2 oz) chopped fresh mushrooms
30 ml (2 tbsp) Oregano Parsley Pesto (p.158) or other pesto
    sauce
salt (optional)
black pepper to taste

1. Heat olive oil over moderate heat in a large soup pan and sauté onion until tender, about 4 minutes.

2. Add tomatoes, carrots, cabbage, courgettes, water, spring onions, potatoes and mushrooms. Cover and cook at a gentle boil for 18 minutes or until vegetables are tender. Add pesto, salt, if using, and pepper and turn off heat. Serve.

Greek Lentil Soup

Lentils are one of the oldest cultivated foods. They're extremely versatile, tasty, and packed with nutrition – high in vegetable protein, iron, minerals and vitamins A and B. The Chilean lentil is brown, yellow or grey and the Persian lentil is red-orange. All are good. Serve this hearty soup with Garlic Bread (p. 164). Greek Lentil Soup can be refrigerated for up to 3 days. When reheating, you may want to add extra liquid to compensate for thickening.

225 g (8 oz) dried lentils, sorted
1 bay leaf
12 black peppercorns
2.5 ml (¹/₂ tsp) dried thyme
2.5 ml (¹/₂ tsp) dried marjoram
90 ml (6 tbsp) extra-virgin olive oil
1 onion, chopped
2 cloves garlic, crushed
2 carrots, chopped
2 sticks of celery, chopped
175 g (6 oz) canned chopped tomatoes
1.5 litres (2³/₄ pints) water
3 low-fat vegetable stock cubes, crumbled

1. Pour lentils into a colander and rinse with cool water.
2. Tie bay leaf, peppercorns, thyme and marjoram in a small square of muslin.
3. Heat olive oil in a large, heavy soup pan over moderate heat and sauté onion and garlic for 2 minutes. Add carrots and celery and cook for 1 minute more.
4. Add lentils and muslin square to soup pan. Stir in tomatoes, water and stock cubes. Bring soup to the boil over moderate heat. Reduce heat to low and simmer, covered, for 1¹/₄ hours or until lentils are tender. Discard herbs and muslin.

Variation
Add 225 g (8 oz) diced cooked chicken 15 minutes before the cooking time is completed.

serves 6

preparation time
20 minutes

cooking time
1 hour and 20 minutes

nutrient analysis
Calories per serving: 220
Protein: 9 gm
Carbohydrates: 14 gm
Dietary fibre: 4.1 gm
Cholesterol: 1 mg
Total fat: 15 gm (137 cal)
Sat fat: 2.4 gm (21 cal)
Poly fat: 1.6 gm (14 cal)
Mono fat: 10.6 gm (95 cal)

Vegetable Soups

Fresh vegetables are especially good in soups. Choose vegetables that are in season for the most flavourful soups. When served with reduced-fat cheeses and wholemeal breads there is no meal that is more satisfying and simple to prepare.

Gazpacho

serves 6

preparation time
30 minutes

cooking time
(croutons) 10 minutes

nutrient analysis
Calories per serving: 404
Protein: 8.5 gm
Carbohydrates: 48 gm
Dietary fibre: 3.8 gm
Cholesterol: 0 mg
Total fat: 21 gm (189 cal)
Sat fat: 3.1 gm (28 cal)
Poly fat: 1.7 gm (14.6 cal)
Mono fat: 13 gm (117 cal)

Gazpacho, which was created in the southern Spanish province of Andalusia, is sometimes called 'the salad soup'. Since the climate in Andalusia is particularly hot, the popularity of gazpacho was greatly heightened by the fact that it is traditionally served icy cold. Gazpacho can be served as the first course of a formal meal or as a main dish.

In this recipe, basic Gazpacho is served with a bowl of crunchy croûtons. Small bowls of garnishes such as chopped red onions, cucumbers, seeded green, red and yellow peppers and canned jalapeño peppers, hard-boiled eggs and coriander leaves can also accompany the Gazpacho.

2 medium cucumbers, peeled and chopped
5 medium tomatoes, peeled and chopped
1 large red onion, chopped
1 medium green pepper, seeded and chopped
2 cloves garlic, crushed
100 g (4 oz) stale French bread, crusts removed, crumbled
1 litre (1³/₄ pints) cold water
45 ml (3 tbsp) red wine vinegar
30 ml (2 tbsp) lemon juice
60 ml (4 tbsp) olive oil
15 ml (1 tbsp) tomato purée

Croûtons
50 g (2 oz) bread, crusts removed and cut into 5-mm
(¹/₄inch) cubes
60 ml (4 tbsp) olive oil

1. In a large glass bowl, combine cucumbers, tomatoes, onion, green pepper, garlic and crumbled bread.
2. Stir in water, vinegar and lemon juice.
3. Ladle the mixture into a blender and process until reduced to a purée. Return purée to the bowl, and beat in olive oil and tomato purée with a wire whisk.

4. Tightly cover bowl and refrigerate for a minimum of 2 hours. Whisk again immediately before serving.

5. Make croûtons while soup is chilling. Heat 60 ml (4 tbsp) olive oil in a frying pan over moderate heat. Drop in bread cubes and cook, turning frequently with a wide spatula. Cook until crisp and lightly browned on all sides. Serve in a separate dish; sprinkle on the soup when served.

Variations

★ Add herbs such as parsley, mint, oregano or chives after blending the gazpacho and before chilling it.

★ Add 100 g (4 oz) shredded ham, lean roast beef or crab meat just before serving.

Tomato Herb Soup

This fragrant soup is based on a recipe that is traditionally prepared in a frying pan in Provence. It features thyme, which is thought to be a tonic and stimulant, as well as marjoram, which is thought to cleanse the body of impurities. Serve with Chef's Salad Valencia (p. 63).

60 ml (4 tbsp) olive oil
3 medium onions
4 medium tomatoes, chopped
3 cloves garlic, crushed
1 bay leaf
5 ml (1 tsp) dried thyme
3.75 ml (³/₄ tsp) dried marjoram
1.25 ml (¹/₄ tsp) black pepper
2 litres (3¹/₂ pints) water
8 slices French bread, toasted in oven
50 g (2 oz) grated Parmesan cheese

1. Heat olive oil in large, heavy soup pan over moderate heat and sauté onions until lightly browned. Add tomatoes and cook for 5 minutes more.

2. Raise heat to high and add garlic, bay leaf, thyme, marjoram, pepper and water. Bring to the boil, reduce heat to moderate and cook for 15 minutes.

3. Purée soup, in batches, in blender or food processor, or force through a food mill.

4. Return soup to pan and reheat soup to boiling over high heat. Place two slices of toasted bread in each serving bowl. Ladle soup over bread and top with cheese.

serves 4

preparation time

15 minutes

cooking time

25 minutes

nutrient analysis

Calories per serving: 400
Protein: 13 gm
Carbohydrates: 46 gm
Dietary fibre: 4 gm
Cholesterol: 9.9 mg
Total fat: 17.7 gm (159 cal)
Sat fat: 4.4 gm (40 cal)
Poly fat: 1.4 gm (12 cal)
Mono fat: 11 gm (100 cal)

Fish Soups and Stews

Seafood soups and stews are low in fat and rich in protein, potassium and phosphorus. Large, round or oval pans or roasting tins that are no more than 15 cm (6 inches) deep with a non-stick surface are the best choices to use while preparing these soups and stews. Crusty bread, green salad and fruit desserts are ideal accompaniments to these dishes. See On the Side, the chapter with recipes for making rouille, a fiery sauce to serve as an accompaniment to fish soups.

Cod Soup

You can use either fresh or frozen cod in this easy-to-prepare, inexpensive soup. Serve it with French bread and a bowl of Parmesan cheese to sprinkle on top. A salad of apple chunks, diced celery and seedless grapes dressed with One Egg Blender Mayonnaise (p. 146) makes a good accompaniment.

serves 4

preparation time

20 minutes

cooking time

35 minutes

nutrient analysis

Calories per serving: 537
Protein: 49 gm
Carbohydrates: 38 gm
Dietary fibre: 3.3 gm
Cholesterol: 70 mg
Total fat: 19 gm (171 cal)
Sat fat: 2.7 gm (24 cal)
Poly fat: 3 gm (27 cal)
Mono fat: 11.6 gm (104 cal)

60 ml (4 tbsp) olive oil
100 g (4 oz) chopped onion
2 cloves garlic, crushed
397 g (14 oz) can chopped tomatoes, drained, juice reserved
60 ml (4 tbsp) finely chopped fresh parsley
1 bay leaf
5 ml (1 tsp) dried thyme
1.25 ml (¼ tsp) black pepper
1.1 litres (2 pints) water
125 ml (4 fl oz) dry white wine
5 ml (1 tsp) grated orange rind
4 medium potatoes, well scrubbed and cut into 2.5 cm (1 inch) cubes
675 g (1½ lb) fresh or frozen cod fillets, cut into 1 cm (½ inch) cubes (thaw frozen fish in refrigerator)

1. Heat olive oil in large, heavy soup pan over moderate heat and sauté onion for 5 minutes or until lightly browned. Add garlic and cook for 1 minute more.
2. Stir in tomatoes. Add parsley, bay leaf, thyme and pepper. Cook for 10 minutes until most of the liquid has evaporated from the tomatoes.
3. Raise heat to high, add water, reserved tomato juice, wine, orange rind, potatoes and fish, and bring to the boil.
4. Reduce heat to moderate, cover and cook for about 15 minutes until potatoes are just tender.

Mediterranean Bouillabaisse

Mediterranean bouillabaisse was named after the earthen-ware pot in which it was cooked by fishermen who prepared their fresh catch and made it go further by adding water, olive oil and lemon juice. Traditionally, bouillabaisse is a combination of several varieties of fish, which can be sea or fresh-water fish. Serve with Basic Rouille (p. 159), a fiery sauce that is added at the table. Garnish with croûtons and accompany with lemon wedges.

125 ml (4 fl oz) extra-virgin olive oil
2 medium onions, thinly sliced
2 small potatoes, peeled and diced
2 small carrots, diced
1 stick of celery, chopped
3 celery tops, chopped
60 ml (4 tbsp) finely chopped fresh parsley
1 clove garlic, crushed
4 peeled ripe or canned tomatoes, chopped
2 litres (3¹/₂ pints) water
1.25 ml (¹/₄ tsp) black pepper
1 large bay leaf
60 ml (4 tbsp) dry white wine
900 ml (2 lb) fish (choose monkfish, John Dory, gurnard,
    cod or red mullet, washed, scaled and cut into serving-size
    pieces)
50 g (2 oz) plain flour
90 g (3¹/₂ oz) raw long-grain rice
1.25 ml (¹/₄ tsp) powdered saffron
40 ml (2¹/₂ tbsp) lemon juice

1. Heat olive oil in a large, heavy soup pan over moderate heat and sauté onions, potatoes, carrots, celery, celery tops, parsley, garlic and tomatoes until almost soft, about 15 minutes.
2. Raise heat to high, add water, pepper and bay leaf, and bring to the boil.
3. Add wine, reduce heat and simmer 20 minutes.
4. Sprinkle fish with flour. Wrap fish in a 90-cm (36-inch) square of muslin and add to pan. Simmer for 10 minutes.
5. Remove muslin and fish with two large spoons and place on a platter to cool.
6. Add rice and saffron to pan and simmer for 25 minutes more until rice is cooked.
7. Untie muslin, remove and discard any skin and bones, then return fish to pan. Add lemon juice and serve.

serves 6

preparation time
20 minutes

cooking time
1 hour

nutrient analysis

Calories per serving: 539
Protein: 45 gm
Carbohydrates: 39 gm
Dietary fibre: 3.5 gm
Cholesterol: 63 mg
Total fat: 23 gm (209 cal)
Sat fat: 3.3 gm (30 cal)
Poly fat: 3.3 gm (30 cal)
Mono fat: 15 gm (134 cal)

SALADS

Mangetout and Carrot Salad

serves 6

preparation time

20 minutes + 2 hours chilling time

cooking time

5–7 minutes

nutrient analysis

Calories per serving: 227
Protein: 4 gm
Carbohydrates: 14 gm
Dietary fibre: 8 gm
Cholesterol: 0 mg
Total fat: 18 gm (165 cal)
Sat fat: 2.6 gm (24 cal)
Poly fat: 1.6 gm (15 cal)
Mono fat: 13 gm (119 cal)

Carrots, radishes, spring onions and mangetout are accented with dill in this refreshing, chilled salad. Serve with Easy Baked Chicken Breasts (p. 70) and Lemon-Dill Rice (p. 108).

250 ml (8 fl oz) water
675 g (1½ lb) mangetout, topped, tailed and strings removed
4 carrots, peeled and cut into matchstick-sized pieces
75 g (3 oz) spring onions, finely chopped
2.5 ml (½ tsp) dried dill
30 ml (2 tbsp) finely chopped fresh parsley
75 ml (5 tbsp) wine vinegar
125 ml (4 fl oz) mild, light-flavoured olive oil
1.25 ml (¼ tsp) black pepper
50 g (2 oz) radishes, thinly sliced

1. Bring water to the boil in a saucepan containing a vegetable steamer. Add mangetout, cover and steam for 3–4 minutes or until just crisp-tender. Run under cold water, drain and put in salad bowl.
2. Steam carrots in steamer for 2–3 minutes. Remove from steamer and add to salad bowl. Chill.
3. Combine spring onions, dill, parsley, vinegar and olive oil in a blender and process until smooth. Season with pepper and pour over mangetout and carrots. Cover and chill for several hours.
4. Add radishes before serving.

Asparagus Vinaigrette

When buying asparagus, look for firm, well-rounded spears of similar size. Avoid spears with open or wilted tips. Cut or snap off the tough white ends before using. Serve with Baked Fish Steaks (p. 74) and Sautéed Potatoes with Red Pepper Oil (p. 96).

900 g (2 lb) fresh asparagus
90 ml (6 tbsp) extra-virgin olive oil
30 ml (2 tbsp) lemon juice
1.25 ml (¼ tsp) black pepper
1 clove garlic, crushed
15 ml (1 tbsp) finely chopped onion or spring onions
15 ml (1 tbsp) finely chopped fresh parsley

1. Microwave or steam asparagus for 5 minutes, just until barely tender.
2. In a small bowl, combine oil, lemon juice, black pepper, garlic, onion and parsley. Mix well and chill.
3. Arrange asparagus on serving dish and pour dressing over spears to cover well.

Variation
Omit the onion, parsley and lemon. Add 30 ml (2 tbsp) wine vinegar and 2.5 ml (½ tsp) mustard powder.

---

serves 4

Q

preparation time
10 minutes

cooking time
5 minutes

nutrient analysis
Calories per serving: 238
Protein: 6 gm
Carbohydrates: 11 gm
Dietary fibre: 2.8 gm
Cholesterol: 0 mg
Total fat: 21 gm (189 cal)
Sat fat: 3 gm (27 cal)
Poly fat: 2 gm (18 cal)
Mono fat: 15 gm (135 cal)

serves 5

Q

preparation time

20 minutes

nutrient analysis

Calories per serving: 178
Protein: 1.4 gm
Carbohydrates: 12.8 gm
Dietary fibre: 3.2 gm
Cholesterol: 0 mg
Total fat: 15 gm (131 cal)
Sat fat: 2 gm (19 cal)
Poly fat: 1.3 gm (12 cal)
Mono fat: 11 gm (95 cal)

Shredded Carrot-Turnip Slaw

Carrots, turnips, cabbage, apples and radishes are marinated in a honey-vinaigrette dressing. Buy turnips that are firm, smooth and fairly round. Avoid those that have obvious fibrous roots and yellow, wilted tops.

2 large carrots, shredded
1 medium turnip, peeled and shredded
350 g (12 oz) green cabbage, shredded
1 red apple, cored and thinly sliced
75 g (3 oz) radishes, sliced
2 spring onions, thinly sliced
75 ml (5 tbsp) mild, light-flavoured olive oil
60 ml (4 tbsp) cider vinegar
5 ml (1 tsp) honey
2.5 ml (½ tsp) black pepper

1. Combine carrots, turnip, cabbage, apple, radishes and spring onions in a salad bowl.
2. Mix oil, vinegar, honey and pepper in a small bowl with a wire whisk. Pour over vegetables and chill for several hours before serving.

serves 4

Q

preparation time

10 minutes

cooking time

15 minutes

nutrient analysis

Calories per serving: 136
Protein: 0.7 gm
Carbohydrates: 3.8 gm
Dietary fibre: 0.8 gm
Cholesterol: 0 mg
Total fat: 14 gm (124 cal)
Sat fat: 1.9 gm (18 cal)
Poly fat: 1.3 gm (11 cal)
Mono fat: 10 gm (90 cal)

Tri-colour Pepper Salad

A simple pepper salad is a delightful garnish for any meal. It can be eaten warm or prepared in advance and served cold.

60 ml (4 tbsp) mild, light-flavoured olive oil
1 red pepper, seeded and cut into 5 cm (2 inch) strips
1 yellow pepper, seeded and cut into 5 cm (2 inch) strips
1 green pepper, seeded and cut into 5 cm (2 inch) strips
2 cloves garlic, crushed
5 ml (1 tsp) dried basil
15 ml (1 tbsp) chopped fresh parsley
1.25 ml (¼ tsp) salt (optional)
1.25 ml (¼ tsp) black pepper

1. Heat olive oil in a large frying pan over moderate heat. Add peppers and garlic and sauté for 15 minutes until soft.
2. When peppers are soft, add basil, salt (if using) and black pepper. Mix well and serve at room temperature or chilled.

Tomatoes with Parsley

Parsley is the most popular of all cooking herbs and appears in all Mediterranean cuisines. When you bring fresh parsley home from the market, rinse it, shake it, and wrap it in absorbent kitchen paper, then store in a jar or polythene bag in the refrigerator. Parsley stored in this manner will stay fresh for two weeks or more. Serve Tomatoes with Parsley as a side dish with Linguine with Oil and Garlic (p. 110).

1 clove garlic, crushed
125 ml (4 fl oz) extra-virgin olive oil
45 ml (3 tbsp) wine vinegar
1.25 ml (¼ tsp) salt (optional)
1.25 ml (¼ tsp) black pepper
100 g (4 oz) fresh parsley leaves
40 g (1½ oz) Parmesan cheese
4 medium tomatoes, thinly sliced

1. Process garlic, olive oil, vinegar, salt, if using, and pepper in a blender or food processor or shake well in a small, covered jar.
2. Put parsley in a bowl and pour dressing over. Add Parmesan cheese and mix well.
3. Put tomato slices in a glass bowl. Add parsley-cheese mixture and toss well.

Variation
Omit cheese. Add 225 g (8 oz) steamed green beans and 3 finely chopped spring onions.

serves 6

Q

preparation time

10 minutes

nutrient analysis

Calories per serving: 227
Protein: 5.1 gm
Carbohydrates: 7.5 gm
Dietary fibre: 3.0 gm
Cholesterol: 6.6 mg
Total fat: 21 gm (187 cal)
Sat fat: 4.1 gm (38 cal)
Poly fat: 1.6 gm (15 cal)
Mono fat: 14 gm (126 cal)

Broccoli Salad

serves 4

Q

preparation time

2 minutes

cooking time

5 minutes

nutrient analysis

Calories per serving: 246
Protein: 8 gm
Carbohydrates: 12 gm
Dietary fibre: 5.6 gm
Cholesterol: 25 mg
Total fat: 20 gm (180 cal)
Sat fat: 6.2 gm (57 cal)
Poly fat: 1.5 gm (14 cal)
Mono fat: 11.3 gm (102 cal)

Blanched broccoli is mixed with onion rings, mushrooms and feta cheese in a lemon-flavoured dressing. Serve with Pan-Sautéed Fish (p. 80).

450 g (1 lb) broccoli florets
1 onion, sliced and separated into rings
50 g (2 oz) sliced fresh mushrooms
100 g (4 oz) feta cheese, crumbled into small pieces
45 ml (3 tbsp) lemon juice
60 ml (4 tbsp) olive oil
1 clove garlic, crushed
2.5 ml (½ tsp) dried oregano
1.25 ml (¼ tsp) black pepper

1. Drop the broccoli into boiling water over high heat and quickly return water to boil. Drain and chill.
2. Toss broccoli with onion, mushrooms and cheese.
3. Process lemon juice, olive oil, garlic, oregano and pepper in a blender or food processor or mix in a small bowl using a wire whisk. Pour over broccoli mixture, toss and serve.

Israeli Salad

serves 4

Q

preparation time

15 minutes

nutrient analysis

Calories per serving: 144
Protein: 1 gm
Carbohydrates: 5.8 gm
Dietary fibre: 1.9 gm
Cholesterol: 0 mg
Total fat: 13.8 gm (124 cal)
Sat fat: 2 gm (18 cal)
Poly fat: 1.3 gm (11 cal)
Mono fat: 10 gm (90 cal)

Salad is served with almost every Israeli meal including breakfast. The ingredients for this dish are frequently kept on the tables in kibbutz dining halls so that members of the collective community can make their own fresh salads. Serve with Baked Fish Steaks (p. 74) for a quick and easy supper.

2 ripe tomatoes, chopped
1 cucumber, peeled and chopped
1 green pepper, seeded and chopped
30 ml (2 tbsp) chopped fresh parsley
60 ml (4 tbsp) extra-virgin olive oil
45 ml (3 tbsp) lemon juice
1.25 ml (¼ tsp) black pepper
1.25 ml (¼ tsp) salt (optional)

1. Mix chopped tomatoes, cucumber, green pepper and parsley in a large bowl.
2. Add olive oil and toss salad.
3. Add lemon juice, pepper and salt, if using, and toss again to mix well.

Puerto Rican Avocado Salad

Since avocados are also high in monounsaturates, you'll be getting a double portion of monounsaturate calories by eating this citrus-accented tropical salad. Serve with Grilled Fish Steaks (p. 74).

3 ripe avocados
175 g (6 oz) drained pineapple chunks in natural juice
125 ml (4 fl oz) mild, light-flavoured olive oil
60 ml (4 tbsp) wine vinegar
1.25 ml (¹/₄ tsp) lime or lemon juice
pinch of black pepper
5 ml (1 tsp) sugar (optional)
1 small radicchio lettuce, separated into leaves, rinsed and drained
2 oranges, peeled and separated into segments

1. Cut avocados in half, lengthways. Remove stones and carefully scoop out pulp. Reserve shells.
2. Cut avocado pulp into 1-cm (¹/₂-inch) pieces and mix with pineapple chunks in a medium bowl.
3. In a small bowl mix olive oil, vinegar, lime juice, pepper and sugar, if using, with a wire whisk until well mixed. Pour over avocado and pineapple chunks.
4. Spoon salad back into empty shells. Place each filled shell on a bed of lettuce leaves on individual salad plates. Garnish with orange segments. Refrigerate until ready to serve.

serves 6

Q

preparation time

15 minutes

nutrient analysis

Calories per serving: 366
Protein: 3 gm
Carbohydrates: 19 gm
Dietary fibre: 5 gm
Cholesterol: 0 mg
Total fat: 33 gm (299 cal)
Sat fat: 4.8 gm (43 cal)
Poly fat: 3.4 gm (30 cal)
Mono fat: 23 gm (206 cal)

Cauliflower Salad

serves 4

preparation time

20 minutes

cooking time

12 minutes + 2 hours
marinating time

nutrient analysis

Calories per serving: 155
Protein: 3.8 gm
Carbohydrates: 6.5 gm
Dietary fibre: 2.7 gm
Cholesterol: 0 mg
Total fat: 14 gm (124 cal)
Sat fat: 2 gm (17 cal)
Poly fat: 1.2 gm (11 cal)
Mono fat: 10 gm (90 cal)

Cauliflower is marinated in a zesty paprika dressing and sprinkled with chopped egg white and parsley. Serve with grilled boneless chicken breasts and Courgette Fritters (p. 99).

1 small cauliflower, cut into florets with stems removed
10 ml (2 tsp) lemon juice
60 ml (4 tbsp) extra-virgin olive oil
30 ml (2 tbsp) wine vinegar
1 clove garlic, crushed
5 ml (1 tsp) paprika
pinch of cayenne pepper
45 ml (3 tbsp) hard-boiled egg white, finely chopped
15 ml (1 tbsp) chopped fresh parsley

1.   Place cauliflower in a saucepan with 2.5 cm (1 inch) boiling water. Add lemon juice. Cover and cook over low heat for 12 minutes. Drain and cool.

2.   Process olive oil, vinegar, garlic, paprika and cayenne in a blender or food processor, or mix in a small bowl with a wire whisk until well blended.

3.   Pour over cooled cauliflower and marinate for 2 hours. Garnish with egg white and parsley and serve.

Greek Salad

A traditional Greek Salad is easy to assemble. Try serving it on pita rounds for a special treat for lunch or a light supper.

1 clove garlic, cut in half
1 Cos lettuce or 225 g (8 oz) mixed salad greens, rinsed, dried and cut into 5-cm (2-inch) pieces
8 red radishes, cut in half
10 black olives, rinsed
1 red onion, thinly sliced and divided into rings
1 green pepper, seeded and thinly sliced
1 medium cucumber, thinly sliced
1 ripe medium tomato, cut in wedges
1.25 ml (¹/₄ tsp) black pepper
1.25 ml (¹/₄ tsp) dried dill
2.5 ml (¹/₂ tsp) dried oregano
30 ml (2 tbsp) red wine vinegar
125 ml (4 fl oz) extra-virgin olive oil

1. Rub a large salad bowl with the cut garlic clove.
2. Place lettuce or salad greens, radishes, olives, onion, green pepper, cucumber and tomato in bowl. Add black pepper, dill, oregano and vinegar. Toss.
3. Add olive oil and toss again.

Variation
Garnish with anchovies and feta cheese.

serves 4

Q

preparation time

20 minutes

nutrient analysis

Calories per serving: 283
Protein: 2.2 gm
Carbohydrates: 88 gm
Dietary fibre: 2.8 gm
Cholesterol: 0 mg
Total fat: 28 gm (258 cal)
Sat fat: 4 gm (36 cal)
Poly fat: 2.5 gm (23 cal)
Mono fat: 21 gm (188 cal)

serves 4

Q

preparation time

10 minutes + potato boiling
time

nutrient analysis

Calories per serving: 250
Protein: 3 gm
Carbohydrates: 29 gm
Dietary fibre: 3.1 gm
Cholesterol: 0 mg
Total fat: 15 gm (136 cal)
Sat fat: 2 gm (19 cal)
Poly fat: 1.3 gm (12 cal)
Mono fat: 10.6 gm (96 cal)

Syrian Potato Salad

In this salad, potatoes are tossed with olive oil, lemon juice
and onions, then topped with olives, tomatoes and mint.
Serve with grilled chicken.

450 g (1 lb) potatoes, boiled, peeled and cubed
60 ml (4 tbsp) olive oil
juice of 1 lemon
1 medium onion, finely chopped
1.25 ml (¹/₄ tsp) black pepper
15 ml (1 tbsp) dried mint
15 ml (1 tbsp) chopped fresh parsley
8 black olives, rinsed and drained
2 ripe medium tomatoes, sliced

1. Toss warm potatoes with olive oil.
2. Add lemon juice, onion, pepper and mint.
3. When cool, garnish with parsley, olives and tomatoes.

Quick Bean Salad

This easy-to-make salad is made with canned beans and
can be garnished with black olives and lemon slices. Serve
with Citrus-Herb Roast Chicken (p. 69).

2 (396-g/14-oz) cans butter beans or cannellini beans, well
*   drained*
60 ml (4 tbsp) olive oil
60 ml (4 tbsp) lemon juice
15 ml (1 tbsp) wine vinegar
1.25 ml (¹/₄ tsp) salt (optional)
1.25 ml (¹/₄ tsp) black pepper
15 ml (1 tbsp) Dijon mustard
30 ml (2 tbsp) chopped fresh parsley
1.25 ml (¹/₄ tsp) dried oregano
1 red onion, thinly sliced
1 ripe tomato, sliced
1 green pepper, seeded and sliced

serves 4

Q

preparation time

20 minutes

nutrient analysis

Calories per serving: 380
Protein: 16.5 gm
Carbohydrates: 49 gm
Dietary fibre: 0.8 gm
Cholesterol: 0 mg
Total fat: 15 gm (134 cal)
Sat fat: 2 gm (18 cal)
Poly fat: 1.3 gm (11 cal)
Mono fat: 10 gm (90 cal)

1. Put drained beans in a large bowl.
2. Combine olive oil, lemon juice, vinegar, salt, if using,
pepper and mustard. Mix with a whisk. Pour over beans
and mix well.
3. Add parsley, oregano, red onion, tomato and green
pepper. Toss well.

Dill and Lentil Salad

Make lentil salad by dressing freshly cooked lentils with a lemon-oil dressing, then tossing them with tomatoes and spring onions. It is one of the most delicious ways to eat this excellent source of protein. Serve with Citrus-Herb Roast Chicken (p. 69).

225 g (8 oz) dried brown lentils, sorted and rinsed
500 ml (17 fl oz) water
1 large carrot, thinly sliced
1 medium onion, chopped
1 clove garlic, crushed
60 ml (4 tbsp) olive oil
juice of 1 lemon
1.25 ml (¼ tsp) black pepper
10 ml (2 tsp) chopped fresh dill or 2.5 ml (½ tsp) dried dill
1 medium ripe tomato, chopped
3 chopped spring onions

1. Simmer lentils in water in a large saucepan over low heat for 20 minutes until cooked. Add carrot and cook for 5 minutes more until lentils and carrot are soft.
2. In a medium frying pan sauté onion and garlic in 2 tablespoons of the olive oil for 5 minutes or until soft. Combine with lentils and carrot.
3. Add lemon juice, remaining olive oil, pepper and dill to lentils.
4. Toss with chopped tomatoes and spring onions and serve warm or refrigerate and serve cold.

serves 4

preparation time

15 minutes

cooking time

30 minutes

nutrient analysis

Calories per serving: 201
Protein: 5 gm
Carbohydrates: 16.8 gm
Dietary fibre: 4 gm
Cholesterol: 0 mg
Total fat: 14 gm (125 cal)
Sat fat: 2 gm (18 cal)
Poly fat: 1.2 gm (11 cal)
Mono fat: 10 gm (90 cal)

Salad Niçoise

serves 4

___

preparation time

30 minutes + potato cooking
and bean steaming time

___

nutrient analysis

Calories per serving: 431
Protein: 24 gm
Carbohydrates: 36.5 gm
Dietary fibre: 5.4 gm
Cholesterol: 20 mg
Total fat: 24 gm (215 cal)
Sat fat: 3.2 gm (29 cal)
Poly fat: 2.5 gm (23 cal)
Mono fat: 15 gm (145 cal)

Salad Niçoise, a classic French salad, is an inspired blend of tuna, green beans, potatoes and olives.

450 g (1 lb) green beans, topped, tailed and cut into 2.5-cm (1-inch) pieces
3 medium red potatoes, peeled, cooked and sliced
90 ml (6 tbsp) extra-virgin olive oil
15 ml (1 tbsp) wine vinegar
1 clove garlic, crushed
5 ml (1 tsp) Dijon mustard
1.25 ml (¼ tsp) salt (optional)
1.25 ml (¼ tsp) black pepper
1.25 ml (¼ tsp) dried thyme
2.5 ml (½ tsp) dried basil
2.5 ml (½ tsp) dried tarragon
4 large leaves Cos lettuce, rinsed and drained
1 green pepper, seeded and thinly sliced
2 sticks of celery, thinly sliced
175 g (6 oz) baby tomatoes, cut in half
198 g (7 oz) can tuna, preferably yellow-fin, packed in water, drained
6 stuffed green olives, rinsed
6 black olives, rinsed and drained
1 small red onion, thinly sliced and separated into rings
30 ml (2 tbsp) chopped fresh parsley
2 spring onions, chopped
3 hard-boiled egg whites, quartered

1. Steam green beans for 5–10 minutes until crisp tender. Drain and refrigerate.
2. Boil potatoes until tender; drain, slice and refrigerate.
3. Whisk olive oil, vinegar, garlic, mustard, salt, if using, pepper, thyme, basil and tarragon in a small bowl until well blended; or put dressing ingredients in a small jar and shake well. Refrigerate while assembling salad.
4. Arrange lettuce, beans, potatoes, green peppers, celery and tomatoes in a salad bowl. Flake tuna with a fork over salad. Top with olives, onion, parsley, spring onions and egg whites.
5. Mix the olive oil dressing well and drizzle over salad.

Variation
Add 25–50 g (1–2 oz) anchovies to the salad. We have left them out because of their high sodium content.

Green Bean Salad

Look for green beans that are fresh and bright green. Avoid limp, spindly beans or those bulging with seeds. Serve with Rump Steak with Onion-Mustard Sauce (p. 86) and Mexican Cauliflower (p. 102).

450 g (1 lb) fresh green beans, washed, topped and tailed
  (or frozen beans)
pinch of black pepper
25 g (1 oz) finely chopped red onion
30 ml (2 tbsp) finely chopped fresh parsley
60 ml (4 tbsp) olive oil
30 ml (2 tbsp) wine vinegar or lemon juice

1. Steam green beans for 5–10 minutes until tender but still crisp. (Or beans can be microwaved.) Drain well.
2. Place cooked beans in a flat soup plate or deep serving platter. Sprinkle with pepper, onion and parsley.
3. Drizzle olive oil and vinegar over beans.
4. Refrigerate until chilled, about 30 minutes.

Variation
Slice 2 ripe tomatoes and place on larger platter next to the beans. Double the amount of onions, parsley and dressing and drizzle over the beans and tomatoes. Chill.

serves 4

Q

preparation time

15 minutes + 5–10 minutes
bean steaming time

nutrient analysis

Calories per serving: 164
Protein: 2.4 gm
Carbohydrates: 10.5 gm
Dietary fibre: 2.4 gm
Cholesterol: 0 mg
Total fat: 14 gm (125 cal)
Sat fat: 1.9 gm (18 cal)
Poly fat: 1.3 gm (12 cal)
Mono fat: 10 gm (90 cal)

Rice Salad

This combination of cooked rice, herb dressing, tuna and raw vegetables can be served with One Egg Blender Mayonnaise (p. 146).

serves 4

preparation time

15 minutes
(not including cooking rice)
+ 1 hour standing time

cooking time

5 minutes

nutrient analysis

Calories per serving: 340
Protein: 9 gm
Carbohydrates: 39 gm
Dietary fibre: 0.8 gm
Cholesterol: 7.4 mg
Total fat: 17.5 gm (158 cal)
Sat fat: 2.4 gm (22 cal)
Poly fat: 1.6 gm (14 cal)
Mono fat: 12.4 gm (112 cal)

45 ml (3 tbsp) chopped spring onions
75 ml (5 tbsp) olive oil
225 g (8 oz) cooked rice
15 ml (1 tbsp) wine vinegar
10 ml (2 tsp) lemon juice
1.25 ml (¼ tsp) Dijon mustard
1 clove garlic, crushed
1.25 ml (¼ tsp) dried thyme
pinch of dried tarragon
1.25 ml (¼ tsp) black pepper
15 ml (1 tbsp) chopped fresh parsley
40 g (1½ oz) tuna, preferably yellow-fin, packed in water, drained and flaked
30 ml (2 tbsp) finely chopped green pepper
30 ml (2 tbsp) chopped cucumber
30 ml (2 tbsp) finely chopped carrot
30 ml (2 tbsp) finely chopped gherkin

1. Stir fry spring onions in 30 ml (2 tbsp) of olive oil for 1 minute in a large frying pan. Add cooked rice and stir to coat with oil.
2. While rice cools, combine vinegar, lemon juice, mustard, garlic, thyme, tarragon and pepper in a small bowl. Mix with a wire whisk.
3. Pour dressing over rice and mix well.
4. Stir in parsley, tuna, green pepper, cucumber, carrot and gherkin.
5. Allow to stand at room temperature for 1 hour before serving.

Chef's Salad Valencia

In this delicious Spanish variation of chef's salad, rice is added, and chicken or turkey replace the high cholesterol and high sodium ham and cheese ingredients.

45 ml (3 tbsp) finely chopped onion
15 ml (1 tbsp) finely chopped fresh parsley
2.5 ml (1/2 tsp) dried tarragon
1 clove garlic, cut in half and lightly crushed
250 ml (8 fl oz) extra-virgin olive oil
75 ml (5 tbsp) wine vinegar
225 g (8 oz) cooked rice
1/2 green pepper, seeded and chopped
225 g (8 oz) cooked chicken or turkey, cut into bite-sized
*   pieces*
10 black olives, rinsed and drained
2 small tomatoes, cut in quarters
1 small radicchio lettuce or 4 large leaves Cos lettuce
3 hard-boiled egg whites, quartered

1. In a small bowl, combine onion, parsley, tarragon, garlic, olive oil and vinegar. Mix with a wire whisk. Allow to stand for 25 minutes.
2. In a medium bowl, mix rice with green pepper and chicken or turkey.
3. Remove garlic from dressing. Pour half of the dressing over rice mixture and toss well. Chill in refrigerator for 1 hour.
4. While rice mixture is chilling, marinate olives and tomatoes in 125 ml (4 fl oz) of dressing.
5. Rinse and dry the lettuce leaves and arrange them around the rim of a platter. Mound chilled rice and poultry in the centre of the platter. Scoop olives and tomatoes out of marinade and sprinkle them over rice mixture. Place egg whites around the edges.
6. Drizzle the remaining dressing over the salad.

serves 4

preparation time

30 minutes + 30 minutes standing time for dressing and 1 hour chilling time for salad (not including cooking rice or chicken)

nutrient analysis

Calories per serving: 425
Protein: 13 gm
Carbohydrates: 29 gm
Dietary fibre: 1.4 gm
Cholesterol: 20 mg
Total fat: 29 gm (265 cal)
Sat fat: 4.3 gm (39 cal)
Poly fat: 2.6 gm (24 cal)
Mono fat: 20.7 gm (187 cal)

Turkey Salad

serves 4

preparation time

20 minutes

cooking time

10 minutes + 15 minutes
marinating time

nutrient analysis

Calories per serving: 411
Protein: 26 gm
Carbohydrates: 5 gm
Dietary fibre: 1.5 gm
Cholesterol: 60 mg
Total fat: 32 gm (296 cal)
Sat fat: 5.1 gm (46 cal)
Poly fat: 3.1 gm (28 cal)
Mono fat: 21.4 gm (193 cal)

For this salad, marinated turkey is tossed with a tangy dressing and combined with tomatoes, spring onions and olives. Serve with steamed green beans and marrow tossed with Basic Pesto (p. 158).

4 turkey fillets (450 g/1 lb)
125 ml (4 fl oz) olive oil
3 spring onions, sliced
1.25 ml (¼ tsp) black pepper
45 ml (3 tbsp) wine vinegar
5 ml (1 tsp) Dijon mustard
30 ml (2 tbsp) mayonnaise
175 g (6 oz) baby tomatoes, cut in half
100 g (4 oz) black olives, rinsed
30 ml (2 tbsp) chopped fresh parsley
4 large leaves Cos lettuce, rinsed and drained

1. Sauté turkey fillets in 30 ml (2 tbsp) of the olive oil until lightly browned and tender, approximately 5 minutes on each side. Cool and cut into cubes.

2. Combine turkey cubes and spring onions in a glass bowl and sprinkle with pepper.

3. In a small bowl, mix 30 ml (2 tbsp) of the remaining olive oil and 15 ml (1 tbsp) of the wine vinegar. Stir into turkey mixture. Marinate 15 minutes.

4. While turkey is marinating, combine mustard, mayonnaise and remaining vinegar and oil in a small bowl. Mix with a wire whisk.

5. Pour dressing over marinated turkey and stir. Add baby tomatoes, olives and parsley. Toss and serve on lettuce leaves.

Orange, Onion and Black Olive Salad

Oranges, red onions and black olives are tossed with a spicy lemon and oil dressing for this salad. Serve with Pasta with Chicken and Peppers (p. 114).

2 oranges, peeled, cut into thin slices and seeded
25 g (1 oz) red onion, thinly sliced and separated into rings
8 stoned black olives, rinsed and sliced into rings
5 ml (1 tsp) paprika
1 clove garlic, crushed
5 ml (1 tsp) ground cumin
pinch of cayenne pepper
15 ml (1 tbsp) orange or lemon juice
60 ml (4 tbsp) mild, light-flavoured olive oil
1.25 ml (¼ tsp) white pepper
30 ml (2 tbsp) finely chopped fresh parsley

1. Place oranges, onion and olives in a salad bowl.
2. Process paprika, garlic, cumin, cayenne, orange juice, olive oil and white pepper in a blender or food processor. Alternatively mix in a small bowl with a wire whisk.
3. Pour over oranges, onion and olives and toss to coat. Serve at room temperature or refrigerate until well chilled. Garnish with parsley.

Variation
Omit olives and red onion. Add 4 grated red radishes and 3 diced spring onions.

serves 4

Q

preparation time

15 minutes

nutrient analysis

Calories per serving: 171
Protein: 1.2 gm
Carbohydrates: 10 gm
Dietary fibre: 1.7 gm
Cholesterol: 0 mg
Total fat: 15 gm (136 cal)
Sat fat: 2.1 gm (19 cal)
Poly fat: 1.3 gm (12 cal)
Mono fat: 10.8 gm (97 cal)

POULTRY

Chicken and turkey are loaded with B vitamins and minerals and contain less fat than veal, lamb, beef or pork. Smaller, younger birds have less fat than larger, older birds. Young roasting chickens (1.6–1.8 kg/3^1/$_2$–4 lb) have less than 10 percent fat while older roasting birds have 12 to 18 percent. Poultry white meat has less fat and less cholesterol than dark meat. The breast is the least fatty area and has the highest percentage (63 percent) of edible meat of any chicken part.

The skin contains at least half of the poultry's total saturated fat count; there is a layer of fat under the skin and several large fat deposits near the tail. Consequently, if you remove and discard the skin when you cook poultry, you can cut the fat calories in half.

The skin can be removed either before or after cooking. Whole chickens used for roasting need to have their skins left on as a protective layer to prevent the meat from drying out during the roasting period. Remove the skin when eating after the chicken is cooked.

Cooking tips:

Rinse chicken quickly under cold running water and pat dry with absorbent kitchen paper. It will brown better when dry.

Chicken is done when clear yellow fluid, with no pink traces, appears when the meat is pierced.

Wash all cooking utensils used on chicken, particularly knives and cutting boards, before using on other foods to avoid transferring bacteria.

Garlic Chicken

Despite the large number of garlic cloves used in this popular dish, the flavour of the finished dish is surprisingly subtle. After the chicken is roasted, you can remove the cooked garlic cloves, peel and squeeze them from their hulls, and spread them on slices of toasted bread. When available substitute fresh herbs for the dried herbs in this recipe. Serve with Spinach and Rice (p. 106).

60 ml (4 tbsp) extra-virgin olive oil
900 g (2 lb) chicken cut into serving pieces (about 450 g (1 lb) of meat)
1 medium onion, chopped
4 sticks of celery, chopped
2 medium carrots, chopped
30 ml (2 tbsp) chopped fresh parsley
2 whole heads garlic, separated into unpeeled cloves (about 25 cloves)
60 ml (4 tbsp) dry white wine
60 ml (4 tbsp) water
2.5 ml (¹/₂ tsp) dried thyme
2.5 ml (¹/₂ tsp) dried basil
2.5 ml (¹/₂ tsp) dried rosemary
2.5 ml (¹/₂ tsp) dried oregano

1. Preheat oven to 180°C (350°F) mark 4. Heat olive oil in a heavy frying pan and sauté chicken for about 15 minutes over moderate heat until lightly browned.

2. Put onion, celery, carrots and parsley on the base of a large ovenproof casserole. Layer chicken over vegetables. Tuck garlic cloves between chicken pieces. Pour wine and water over chicken. Sprinkle with thyme, basil, rosemary and oregano.

3. Cover casserole and bake for 1¹/₂ hours. Don't lift the lid until cooking time is completed. Skin chicken before eating.

serves 4

preparation time
20 minutes

cooking time
1³/₄ hours

nutrient analysis

Calories per serving: 355
Protein: 37 gm
Carbohydrates: 12 gm
Dietary fibre: 1.5 gm
Cholesterol: 93.9 mg
Total fat: 18 gm (159 cal)
Sat fat: 3.1 gm (28 cal)
Poly fat: 2.2 gm (19 cal)
Mono fat: 11.4 gm (102 cal)

Chicken Verde

preparation time

15 minutes

cooking time

45 minutes

nutrient analysis

Calories per serving: 544
Protein: 39 gm
Carbohydrates: 7.1 gm
Dietary fibre: 1.9 gm
Cholesterol: 98 mg
Total fat: 40.8 gm (367 cal)
Sat fat: 7 gm (62 cal)
Poly fat: 4.2 gm (38 cal)
Mono fat: 27.7 gm (249 cal)

Smother baked chicken breasts with a pesto-style green sauce. Serve with steamed courgettes and Sautéed Potatoes with Red Pepper Oil (p. 96).

450 g (1 lb) boneless chicken breasts, skinned and cut in
  half (or turkey breast)
150 ml (¼ pint) olive oil
1.25 ml (¼ tsp) black pepper
juice of 1 lemon
2 cloves garlic, cut in half
75 g (3 oz) chopped fresh basil, parsley or a combination
45 ml (3 tbsp) grated Parmesan cheese
30 ml (2 tbsp) pine nuts

1. Preheat oven to 180°C (350°F) mark 4.
2. Rub chicken with 30 ml (2 tbsp) of the olive oil and sprinkle with black pepper. Place chicken in baking dish.
3. Cover and bake for 45 minutes or until lightly browned.
4. While chicken is cooking combine lemon juice, remaining olive oil, garlic, basil or parsley and cheese in a blender or food processor and blend until smooth.
5. Serve chicken covered with green sauce and sprinkled with pine nuts.

Citrus-Herb Roast Chicken

Roast whole chickens are easy to prepare. They make an inexpensive family meal or enough chicken for salads, crêpes, sandwiches and more. This recipe and its variations are made from the same basic cooking method using olive oil with a variety of flavourings. Serve roast chicken with Puffed French 'Fried' Potatoes (p. 103) and Asparagus Vinaigrette (p. 51).

1 × 1.4 kg (3 lb) chicken
2.5 ml (¹/₂ tsp) black pepper
2 cloves garlic, crushed
60 ml (4 tbsp) lemon juice
60 ml (4 tbsp) olive oil
7.5 ml (1¹/₂ tsp) dried thyme

1. Preheat oven to 230°C (450°F) mark 8. Wash chicken inside and out. Pat dry with absorbent kitchen paper. Sprinkle with pepper.
2. Rub chicken with garlic inside and out and place on a rack in a roasting tin, breast-side up.
3. Mix lemon juice and oil together and pour over chicken, rubbing in lightly.
4. Sprinkle thyme over chicken.
5. Reduce oven temperature to 180°C (350°F) mark 4 and put chicken in oven. Baste with pan juices every 15 minutes for about 1¹/₄ hours or until the joints pull away easily. Remove skin before eating.

Orange-Cumin Roast Chicken
Omit lemon juice and thyme. Mix the juice of 1 small orange and 5 ml (1 tsp) powdered cumin with the olive oil. Pour over chicken and rub in lightly; roast.

Calypso Roast Chicken
Omit garlic, lemon juice and thyme. Mix 30 ml (2 tbsp) lime juice with the olive oil. Rub into the chicken, inside and out. Cover the chicken with thin slices of 1 lime and 1 small onion; roast.

Garlic-Paprikash Roast Chicken
Omit lemon juice and thyme. Use 3 crushed cloves of garlic instead of 2 and mix with olive oil. Pour over chicken and rub in lightly. Sprinkle with 10 ml (2 tsp) paprika; roast.

serves 4

preparation time
10 minutes

cooking time
1 hour 15 minutes

nutrient analysis
Calories per serving: 309
Protein: 36 gm
Carbohydrates: 1.3 gm
Dietary fibre: 0 gm
Cholesterol: 94 mg
Total fat: 17.6 gm (158 cal)
Sat fat: 3.1 gm (28 cal)
Poly fat: 2.1 gm (20 cal)
Mono fat: 11.4 gm (103 cal)

Easy Baked Chicken Breasts

serves 4

---

preparation time

15 minutes

---

cooking time

1 hour

---

nutrient analysis

Calories per serving: 430
Protein: 38 gm
Carbohydrates: 30 gm
Dietary fibre: 2.5 gm
Cholesterol: 94 mg
Total fat: 18 gm (159 cal)
Sat fat: 3 gm (28 cal)
Poly fat: 2.2 gm (20 cal)
Mono fat: 11.4 gm (102 cal)

This is a simple casserole for an occasion when you long for something hearty and delicious that requires minimal effort. Serve with broccoli or a green salad with Basic Vinaigrette (p. 144).

450 g (1 lb) boneless chicken breasts, skinned and cut in half (or turkey breast)
4 large potatoes, peeled and cut into eighths
175 g (6 oz) coarsely chopped tomatoes
2.5 ml (¹/₂ tsp) black pepper
5 ml (1 tsp) dried oregano
60 ml (4 tbsp) olive oil
6 large mushrooms, wiped and sliced
15 ml (1 tbsp) chopped fresh parsley

1. Preheat oven to 180° C (350° F) mark 4. Place chicken in an ovenproof casserole. Add potatoes, tomatoes, pepper, oregano, olive oil and mushrooms.

2. Bake, uncovered, for 1 hour. Baste ingredients with sauce from the casserole every 20 minutes. Remove from the oven and sprinkle with parsley.

Chicken Curry

This dish combines chicken with onion, garlic, tomatoes and curry powder. Serve over steamed rice and garnish with toasted almonds. Accompany with spiced apples dusted with nutmeg.

450 g (1 lb) boneless chicken breasts, skinned and cut in
    half (or turkey breast)
50 g (2 oz) plain flour (or oat bran or wheat germ)
1.25 ml (¼ tsp) black pepper
90 ml (6 tbsp) olive oil
100 g (4 oz) chopped onion
1 clove garlic, chopped
75 g (3 oz) chopped green pepper
7.5 ml (1½ tsp) curry powder
2.5 ml (½ tsp) dried thyme
350 g (12 oz) diced fresh or canned chopped tomatoes

1. Preheat oven to 180°C (350°F) mark 4. Pat chicken with absorbent kitchen paper. Combine flour and pepper and sprinkle over both sides of chicken breasts.

2. Heat the olive oil in a large frying pan over moderate heat. Sauté chicken for 15 minutes until lightly browned.

3. Remove from pan with a fish slice and place in a large ovenproof casserole.

4. Add onion, garlic, green pepper, curry powder and thyme to pan and sauté for 5 minutes until lightly browned. Add tomatoes. Stir until heated through.

5. Pour tomato mixture over chicken in casserole. Bake, uncovered, for 30 minutes until chicken is tender.

serves 4

preparation time

15 minutes

cooking time

1¼ hours

nutrient analysis

Calories per serving: 294
Protein: 38 gm
Carbohydrates: 20 gm
Dietary fibre: 2.0 gm
Cholesterol: 94 mg
Total fat: 6.5 gm (59 cal)
Sat fat: 1.6 gm (14 cal)
Poly fat: 1.3 gm (12 cal)
Mono fat: 3 gm (27 cal)

Chicken Couscous

Couscous is a hearty North African main course that is the national dish of Algeria, Tunisia and Morocco. The term couscous refers to both the stew itself and the grain that is part of the dish. Here is a quick version of couscous, flavoured with turmeric and coriander. Serve with pita bread and a fruit salad of hulled strawberries, diced pineapple and melon balls dressed with Balsamic Vinaigrette (p. 144).

serves 4

preparation time

20 minutes

cooking time

1 hour and 5 minutes

nutrient analysis

Calories per serving: 552
Protein: 47 gm
Carbohydrates: 44 gm
Dietary fibre: 2.3 gm
Cholesterol: 94 mg
Total fat: 21.5 gm (194 cal)
Sat fat: 3.4 gm (30 cal)
Poly fat: 2.7 gm (25 cal)
Mono fat: 12 gm (107 cal)

60 ml (4 tbsp) extra-virgin olive oil
450 g (1 lb) boneless chicken breasts, skinned and cut in
* half (or turkey breast)*
125 g (4¹/₂ oz) sliced carrots
75 g (3 oz) sliced onions
125 ml (4 fl oz) water
5 ml (1 tsp) ground coriander
1 clove garlic, crushed
1.25 ml (¹/₄ tsp) cayenne pepper
2.5 ml (¹/₂ tsp) ground turmeric
175 g (6 oz) drained canned chick-peas
100 g (4 oz) sliced courgettes
50 g (2 oz) couscous
40 g (1¹/₂ oz) sultanas
15 ml (1 tbsp) polyunsaturated margarine
125 ml (4 fl oz) boiling water

1. Heat olive oil in heavy frying pan over moderate high heat and cook chicken for 15 minutes until lightly browned on both sides.

2. Stir in carrots, onions, water, coriander, garlic, cayenne and 1.25 ml (¹/₄ tsp) of the turmeric. Bring to the boil. Reduce heat to low and simmer for 25 minutes.

3. Stir in chick-peas and courgettes and simmer for 15 minutes more.

4. Place couscous, sultanas, margarine and remaining turmeric in a medium bowl and pour the boiling water over them. Stir and allow to stand for 5 minutes.

5. Spoon couscous into the centre of a serving dish and arrange chicken and vegetables around it. Pour the pan liquid over the chicken and couscous.

SEAFOOD

Fish

Fish has fewer calories than meat, and it is low in fat and extremely nutritious. An average 100–175 g (4–6 oz) serving supplies one third to one half of the adult daily protein requirements as well as B vitamins, thiamin, riboflavin and niacin. Most fish also provide iodine, copper and iron and, if with the bones such as canned salmon and sardines, supply calcium and phosphorus.

In recent years, studies have indicated that the omega-3 fatty acids found in fish may protect against heart disease by reducing blood cholesterol (particularly LDL) and triglyceride levels. Omega-3's, which are also found in high concentration in the human brain and eye, seem to inhibit the tendency of blood cells to form stroke-related artery-blocking clots. They may also help to ease headaches, premenstrual discomfort, asthma and the inflammation of arthritis.

The highest quantities of omega-3's are found in fish such as salmon with more than 5 percent fat. Sea fish with a high fatty content include spiny dogfish, pilchard, halibut, herring, mackerel, mullet, rainbow trout, salmon, sardines, tuna and sprats and anchovies.

Leaner sea fish include cod, flounder, haddock, monkfish, plaice, scallops and eel. To gain the same number of omega-3's that are in 675 g (1½ lb) of fatter fish, you need to eat 900 g–1.4 kg (2–3 lb) of these leaner fish.

Since environmental concerns and geographical location often limit the availability of specific types of fish, feel free to substitute varieties as you prepare the following recipes.

Cooking Tips

When testing fish for doneness, insert a toothpick into the thickest part of the fish near the backbone and separate the meat from the bone. The fish is done when the flesh is opaque and no longer translucent and flakes readily. You can also test for doneness by pressing on it. If the flesh returns to its original shape after being pressed, the fish is done. Avoid overcooking fish since it tends to dry out rapidly.

When baking fish, try to use a heatproof dish that can double as a serving platter. This will prevent over-handling of the fish and you'll have one less 'fishy' dish to clean.

To remove fish odours from pans after cooking fish, wash with 5 ml (1 tsp) bicarbonate of soda dissolved in 1 litre (1³/₄ pints) water. Rinse with a small amount of vinegar, and then wash with soapy water.

To remove fish odours from your hands, rub with lemon juice and salt or a little vinegar before washing.

Baked or Grilled Fish Steaks

One of the easiest ways to include olive oil on a dinner menu is to use it as a coating for baked or grilled fish steaks. This basic preparation will work either way. Your fish steaks (halibut, salmon or other fish of your choice), should be about 4 cm (1¹/₂ inches) thick. Serve with Simple Vegetable Medley (p. 97).

2 medium fish steaks, 450 g (1 lb)
60 ml (4 tbsp) mild light-flavoured olive oil
1.25 ml (¹/₄ tsp) black pepper
5 ml (1 tsp) dried rosemary

1. Preheat grill (or preheat oven to 200°C (400°F) mark 6) and brush both sides of steaks with olive oil. Season with pepper and rosemary.
2. Grill for 6 minutes on each side or bake in the preheated oven for 15–20 minutes without turning until fish is no longer translucent and flakes easily.

serves 4

Q

preparation time

10 minutes

cooking time

14 minutes if grilled, 20 minutes if baked

nutrient analysis

Calories per serving: 279
Protein: 30.3 gm
Carbohydrates: 0.3 gm
Dietary fibre: 0.3 gm
Cholesterol: 47 mg
Total fat: 16.9 gm (152 cal)
Sat fat: 2.4 gm (22 cal)
Poly fat: 2.2 gm (20 cal)
Mono fat: 11 gm (96 cal)

Fish in Foil

The recipe for baked fish and vegetables is a traditional *Fillets de poisson en papillote* dish, or fish baked in paper. In this version, the fish is smothered with vegetables and cooked in a wine-laced sauce sealed in a foil package. Serve with roast potato wedges with Basic Pesto (p. 158).

675 g (1½ lb) fish fillets
30 ml (2 tbsp) plain flour
pinch of cayenne pepper
60 ml (4 tbsp) olive oil
1 clove garlic, crushed
1 medium onion, thinly sliced
1 medium green pepper, seeded and thinly sliced
100 g (4 oz) mushrooms, thinly sliced
60 ml (4 tbsp) dry white wine
1 large tomato or 175 g (6 oz) drained canned chopped
   tomatoes
15 ml (1 tbsp) lemon juice
60 ml (4 tbsp) tomato purée
1.25 ml (¼ tsp) dried thyme
15 ml (1 tbsp) finely chopped fresh parsley

1. Dip fish in flour and sprinkle with cayenne. Heat olive oil in large frying pan over low heat and sauté garlic for 1 minute. Turn heat up to moderate, add fish and brown for about 3 minutes a side.

2. Tear off a strip of heavy foil 60 cm (24 inches) in length. Remove fish with a slotted spoon or wide spatula and place in the centre of the foil.

3. Preheat oven to 220°C (425°F) mark 7.

4. Sauté onion, peppers and mushrooms in frying pan in remaining oil for 5 minutes until onion slices and peppers are tender. Add wine, tomato, lemon juice, tomato purée and thyme. Bring mixture to the boil and remove from heat.

5. Spoon sauce over fish and seal foil package edges with a double fold, excluding as much air as possible. Place on a baking sheet and bake for 20 minutes.

6. Carefully cut pouch and turn back edges of foil before serving. Garnish with parsley.

serves 4

preparation time
25 minutes

cooking time
40 minutes

nutrient analysis
Calories per serving: 422
Protein: 48 gm
Carbohydrates: 11.4 gm
Dietary fibre: 1.7 gm
Cholesterol: 70 mg
Total fat: 19 gm (170 cal)
Sat fat: 2.7 gm (24 cal)
Poly fat: 2.9 gm (26 cal)
Mono fat: 11.6 gm (104 cal)

Fish Fillets Provençal

serves 4

Q

preparation time

10 minutes

cooking time

30 minutes

nutrient analysis

Calories per serving: 359
Protein: 32 gm
Carbohydrates: 11 gm
Dietary fibre: 1.8 gm
Cholesterol: 47 mg
Total fat: 20.5 gm (185 cal)
Sat fat: 2.9 gm (26 cal)
Poly fat: 2.6 gm (23 cal)
Mono fat: 13.5 gm (122 cal)

Fish fillets are sautéed in olive oil and simmered in a tomato-onion sauce. This dish is traditionally made with cod fillets. Serve with Green Bean Salad (p. 61).

1 medium onion, chopped
75 ml (5 tbsp) mild, light-flavoured olive oil
1 garlic clove, crushed
2 large ripe tomatoes, chopped
5 ml (1 tsp) dried basil
2.5 ml (¹/₂ tsp) dried thyme
15 ml (1 tbsp) finely chopped fresh parsley
1.25 ml (¹/₄ tsp) black pepper
450 g (1 lb) fish fillets
25 g (1 oz) plain flour

1. Sautée onion in medium frying pan in 30 ml (2 tbsp) of the olive oil for 5 minutes or until tender. Add garlic and stir. Add tomatoes, basil, thyme, parsley and pepper. Simmer for 10 minutes.

2. While sauce simmers, dredge fish in flour to coat on both sides.

3. Fry the fish in a large frying pan in the remaining olive oil until lightly browned.

4. Pour sauce over fish in pan and simmer for 15 minutes until fish is no longer translucent and flakes easily.

Mexican Baked Fish

Sauté fish fillets, then cover with a tomato, onion, spice and orange juice sauce and bake. Serve with Olive Bread (p. 165) and a mixed green salad dressed with Cumin Vinaigrette (p. 144).

60 ml (4 tbsp) extra-virgin olive oil
450 g (1 lb) fish fillets
1 medium onion, finely chopped
1 clove garlic, crushed
1 large tomato, chopped
5 ml (1 tsp) dried oregano
pinch of ground cumin
pinch of chilli powder
grated rind of 1 small orange
125 ml (4 fl oz) orange juice
1.25 ml (¼ tsp) black pepper

1. Preheat oven to 190°C (375°F) mark 5.

2. Heat olive oil in large frying pan over moderate heat and shallow fry fillets for 2 minutes a side. Remove fillets with a slotted spoon and set aside.

3. Add onion, garlic, tomato, oregano, cumin, chilli powder and orange rind to pan and stir well. Reduce heat to low and simmer for 20 minutes.

4. Add orange juice to pan.

5. Oil the base and sides of a medium ovenproof casserole. Place half the fish on the base of the casserole and top with half of the tomato-orange sauce. Add the rest of the fish and then rest of the sauce. Sprinkle with pepper. Cover and bake for 30 minutes until bubbly.

serves 4

preparation time
10 minutes

cooking time
1 hour

nutrient analysis
Calories per serving: 309
Protein: 31 gm
Carbohydrates: 7.2 gm
Dietary fibre: 1.3 gm
Cholesterol: 46.7 mg
Total fat: 17 gm (153 cal)
Sat fat: 2.4 gm (22 cal)
Poly fat: 2.2 gm (20 cal)
Mono fat: 11 gm (100 cal)

Baked Fish with Courgettes

serves 4

Q

preparation time

10 minutes

cooking time

20 minutes

nutrient analysis

Calories per serving: 300
Protein: 31 gm
Carbohydrates: 5 gm
Dietary fibre: 2.4 gm
Cholesterol: 47 mg
Total fat: 17 gm (154 cal)
Sat fat: 2.4 gm (22 cal)
Poly fat: 2.3 gm (21 cal)
Mono fat: 11 gm (97 cal)

Courgettes and tomatoes are included with this baked fish dish. Slice some leftover or prebaked potatoes, and sauté in olive oil while the fish cooks, and dinner will be ready!

1 medium courgette, diced
2 medium tomatoes, diced
60 ml (4 tbsp) mild, light-flavoured olive oil
15 ml (1 tbsp) red wine vinegar
15 ml (1 tbsp) finely chopped spring onions
1.25 ml (¼ tsp) black pepper
450 g (1 lb) fish steaks, 2.5 cm (1 inch) thick

1. Preheat oven to 200°C (400°F) mark 6. Sauté courgette and tomatoes in olive oil in a frying pan over moderate heat for 5 minutes. Remove pan from heat and stir in vinegar and spring onions. Sprinkle with pepper.
2. Arrange fish steaks in medium oiled baking dish in one layer. Pour tomato-courgette mixture over fish. Bake for 15 minutes or until the fish is done.

Escabeche

Escabeche is a cold, flavourful fish dish that can be enjoyed as a starter or entrée. In Portugal, it is frequently served as a main course with hot baked potatoes. Once prepared, Escabeche is best when chilled for a least two days before serving. It can be kept in the refrigerator for up to three weeks and will become more delectable with each passing day. Servings given are for entrée.

125 ml (4 fl oz) extra-virgin olive oil
900 g (2 lb) mild, firm, white fish fillets, such as sea bass,
 swordfish or halibut, 1 cm (¹/₂ inch) thick
2 medium onions, peeled and thinly sliced
2 cloves garlic, finely chopped
2 medium carrots, peeled and grated
150 ml (¹/₄ pint) wine vinegar
2 bay leaves, crumbled
2.5 ml (¹/₂ tsp) salt
3.75 ml (³/₄ tsp) black pepper
5 ml (1 tsp) paprika

1. Heat 60 ml (4 tbsp) of the olive oil over moderate heat in a large frying pan and shallow fry fish for about 5 minutes on each side or until it turns white and flakes when tested with a fork. Transfer fish to a medium glass bowl, cool and break into large chunks.

2. Add the rest of the olive oil to the pan and sauté onions and garlic for 3-5 minutes, until softened. Add carrots, vinegar, bay leaves, salt, pepper and paprika. Stir and cook for 2 minutes.

3. Pour vegetable-vinegar mixture over fish and toss lightly to mix.

4. Cover and chill for at least 2 days.

serves 6

---

preparation time

20 minutes

---

cooking time

17 minutes + at least 2 days chilling time

---

nutrient analysis

Calories per serving: 390
Protein: 41 gm
Carbohydrates: 6.3 gm
Dietary fibre: 1.0 gm
Cholesterol: 62 mg
Total fat: 23 gm (203 cal)
Sat fat: 3.2 gm (29 cal)
Poly fat: 3 gm (27 cal)
Mono fat: 15 gm (132 cal)

Pan-Sautéed Fish

serves 4

Q

preparation time

10 minutes

cooking time

10 minutes

nutrient analysis

Calories per serving: 375
Protein: 32 gm
Carbohydrates: 13 gm
Dietary fibre: 0.5 gm
Cholesterol: 46.7 mg
Total fat: 21 gm (193 cal)
Sat fat: 3 gm (28 cal)
Poly fat: 2.6 gm (23 cal)
Mono fat: 14 gm (129 cal)

Serve pan-sautéed fish with tomato sauce, baked new potatoes with Basic Pesto (p. 158) and a Greek Salad (p. 57). Pan-sautéed fish can be kept in a low oven for about 30 minutes until ready to serve.

450 g (1 lb) fish fillets
1.25 ml (¹/₄ tsp) black pepper
50 g (2 oz) plain flour (or 25 g (1 oz) flour and 25 g (1 oz)
*   oat bran)*
1 large clove garlic, cut in half
75 ml (5 tbsp) olive oil
5 ml (1 tsp) dried oregano
1 lemon, quartered

1. Wash fish and pat dry. Sprinkle with pepper and dredge in flour on both sides.
2. Sauté garlic in olive oil in large frying pan over moderate heat. Remove garlic with a slotted spoon and sauté fish for 5 minutes or until brown and crusty to suit your taste on one side. Then turn fish and sauté for 5 minutes more or until fish flakes easily when tested with a fork. Sprinkle with oregano and squeeze lemon juice over fillets before serving.

Variation
For a crustier coating, dip fish first in flour, then in beaten egg white, and finally in breadcrumbs before cooking.

Greek Baked Fish with Vegetables

This recipe, which is a Greek favourite, will provide you with dinner in a dish. In Greece, the baked lemon slices are eaten with their rinds.

900 g (2 lb) whole fish, cleaned and cut into serving portions
30 ml (2 tbsp) lemon juice
125 ml (4 fl oz) extra-virgin olive oil
2 cloves garlic, crushed
3 medium tomatoes, chopped or 1 × 397-g (14-oz) can chopped tomatoes
2 medium onions, thinly sliced
1 green pepper, seeded and chopped
1 large lemon, very thinly sliced and seeded
30 ml (2 tbsp) finely chopped fresh parsley
275 g (10 oz) frozen spinach, thawed or 450 g (1 lb) fresh spinach, washed
1 medium courgette, sliced
2 sticks of celery, chopped
175 ml (6 fl oz) dry white wine
175 ml (6 fl oz) Basic Tomato Sauce (p. 150)
1.25 ml ('/₄ tsp) black pepper
3 large potatoes, peeled and sliced 1 cm ('/₂ inch) thick

1. Rinse fish in cold water and pat dry on absorbent kitchen paper. Rub with lemon juice and 30 ml (2 tbsp) of the olive oil. Return to refrigerator while preparing vegetables.

2. Heat 60 ml (4 tbsp) of the remaining olive oil in a large frying pan over moderate heat. Add garlic, tomatoes, onions, green pepper, lemon slices, parsley, spinach and celery. Stir, reduce heat, cover and simmer for 20 minutes.

3. Preheat oven to 190°C (375°F) mark 5.

4. Add wine, tomato sauce and black pepper to pan. Stir carefully and simmer for 5 minutes more.

5. Place fish in the centre of a large baking tin and pour the vegetables over it. Top with a layer of potato slices and brush lightly with remaining olive oil.

6. Bake, uncovered, for 45 minutes or until fish is done.

serves 6

preparation time

25 minutes

cooking time

1 hour and 10 minutes

nutrient analysis

Calories per serving: 512
Protein: 45 gm
Carbohydrates: 26 gm
Dietary fibre: 5.2 gm
Cholesterol: 62.3 mg
Total fat: 23 gm (208 cal)
Sat fat: 3.3 gm (30 cal)
Poly fat: 3.2 gm (29 cal)
Mono fat: 14.7 gm (133 cal)

Marinated Salmon

serves 4

preparation time

10 minutes + 1 hour
marinating time

cooking time

9 minutes

nutrient analysis

Calories per serving: 460
Protein: 31.4 gm
Carbohydrates: 2.8 gm
Dietary fibre: 0.3 gm
Cholesterol: 56 mg
Total fat: 36 gm (320 cal)
Sat fat: 5.4 gm (48.9 cal)
Poly fat: 4.8 gm (43.1 cal)
Mono fat: 23 gm (205.6 cal)

Marinate salmon steaks, then either grill or bake them. Serve garnished with parsley and lemon slices. Serve with steamed asparagus and Lemon-Dill Rice (p. 108).

450 g (1 lb) salmon fillets
125 ml (4 fl oz) extra-virgin olive oil
60 ml (4 tbsp) orange juice
15 ml (1 tbsp) wine vinegar
45 ml (3 tbsp) finely chopped onion
5 ml (1 tsp) dried tarragon
1.25 ml (¼ tsp) black pepper

1. Place salmon fillets in a large, shallow glass bowl.
2. In a small bowl, combine olive oil, orange juice, vinegar, onion, tarragon and black pepper. Mix with a wire whisk. Pour over salmon. Marinate at room temperature for 30 minutes. Turn salmon and marinate for 30 minutes more.
3. Place salmon, skin-side down, in an oiled grill pan. Baste with marinade and grill for 7–9 minutes, 7.5 cm (3 inches) from heat.
4. Spoon remaining marinade over each serving.

Variation
Bake salmon at 190°C (375°F) mark 5 for 30 minutes or until fish flakes when tested with a fork. Baste with marinade while baking.

Citrus-Marinated Fish

A whole white-fleshed fish of your choice is marinated in fruit juices and then simmered in a piquant tomato sauce. Serve with rice.

1×675 g (1½ lb) sea bass, cleaned, head and tail removed
    or 450 g (1 lb) fish fillets
juice of 1 lemon
juice of 1 orange
1.25 ml (¼ tsp) black pepper
125 ml (4 fl oz) olive oil
1 medium onion, chopped
1 clove garlic, crushed
4 tomatoes, cut in quarters
2 green chillies
pinch of ground cinnamon
pinch of ground cloves
250 ml (8 fl oz) water

1. Place fish in oval glass bowl or baking dish. Combine lemon juice and orange juice and pour over fish. Sprinkle with pepper. Marinate for 1 hour.
2. Purée olive oil, onion, garlic, tomatoes, chillies, cinnamon, cloves and water in a blender or food processor.
3. Simmer purée in a medium saucepan over low heat for 15 minutes.
4. Select a frying pan or saucepan that is large enough to accommodate the entire fish. If this isn't possible, cut the fish in half (and reassemble on the serving platter later when ready to serve). Place one third of the purée on the base of the pan. Add the fish. Top the fish with the rest of the purée.
5. Simmer the fish, over low heat, with lid slightly ajar until fish flakes when tested with a fork, about 5–8 minutes per 450 g (1 lb).

serves 4

preparation time

20 minutes + 1 hour
marinating time

cooking time

Approximately 45 minutes

nutrient analysis

Calories per serving: 532
Protein: 47 gm
Carbohydrates: 12 gm
Dietary fibre: 2.7 gm
Cholesterol: 70 mg
Total fat: 32.9 gm (288 cal)
Sat fat: 4.6 gm (45 cal)
Poly fat: 4 gm (36 cal)
Mono fat: 22 gm (198 cal)

MEAT

Red meat has a relatively high saturated fat count when compared with poultry and fish. Since meat is a major source of saturated fat in the British diet, selecting and preparing it carefully can be a significant factor in lowering total saturated fat intake. A diet that includes too much fatty red meat can increase the risk of heart disease, contribute to obesity, and possibly be linked to some forms of cancer.

On the positive side, meat is an important source of complex protein that contains all the essential amino acid protein building blocks. It provides iron in a form that the body can use easily and is a source of B vitamins and minerals. When we eat more protein than we need from any source, the excess is broken down and burned for energy or stored as fat. Consequently, your goal should be to reduce your daily meat consumption to 75–100 g (3–4 oz) a day rather than cutting it out of your diet completely. Our meat recipes limit each serving to under 100 g (4 oz).

In addition to cutting down on the amount of meat you eat, there are several other steps you can take to reduce the number of saturated fat calories in the meats you consume.

1. Learn how to shop for the lowest fat cuts and grades. As a result of the increased emphasis on a healthier diet, consumption of beef and veal in the United Kingdom has decreased by 25 percent in the past decade. Lamb and mutton consumption is down by 18 percent but pork consumption has remained at more or less the same levels as ten years ago. Total red meat consumption is down by 13 percent. This consumer pressure has led the meat-producing industry to develop leaner cuts of beef, lamb and pork.

The major supermarket chains display lean meat. Look out for 'extra lean', 'ultra lean', 'extra trim' and 'tenderlean' labels, some of which may even carry data as to percentage fat content.

Independent butchers may participate in the 'Lean Choice' scheme, which highlights the availability of lean meat. The scheme requires butchers to offer customers at least six cuts (four of which must be lower-cost items like mince or stewing steak), which are free from visible fat. The scheme is run by the Meat and Livestock Commission in collaboration with the Health

Education Authority, Heartbeat Wales and the Scottish Health Education Group.

2. You need to know which cuts of meat make the healthiest choices.

BEEF: Leanest cuts are topside/silverside, the rump, skirt, thick flank, fillet, extra-lean minced beef and lean stewing beef.

VEAL: All cuts of veal except the breast are lean. However, veal is higher in cholesterol than beef or pork.

LAMB: Lean cuts of lamb include leg of lamb and loin chops. Other fairly lean cuts are loin, shoulder, leg bone steaks, best end cutlets and lamb shanks.

PORK: Relatively lean cuts are loin, loin chops and pork fillet.

3. There are several low-fat cooking techniques you can use to further reduce the fat content of meat once you bring it home.

* Precook meat to get rid of excess fat before adding it to a recipe. Larger pieces of meat or meat cubes can be grilled on a rack in a grill pan, allowing fat to drain off into the pan.
* When cooking with minced meat, brown it in a frying pan by itself and pour off rendered fat before adding other ingredients.

Remember, your goal is to reduce the dangerous saturated fats found in meat and substitute the more healthy monounsaturated fats found in olive oil.

Rump Steak with Onion-Mustard Sauce

serves 4

Q

preparation time

10 minutes

cooking time

15 minutes

nutrient analysis

Calories per serving: 496
Protein: 31 gm
Carbohydrates: 3.8 gm
Dietary fibre: 0.7 gm
Cholesterol: 102.8 mg
Total fat: 40 gm (360 cal)
Sat fat: 12.7 gm (115 cal)
Poly fat: 2.2 gm (20 cal)
Mono fat: 22 gm (196 cal)

In this quick dish, rump steak is sautéed in olive oil and served with an onion-mustard sauce. Serve with Spanish Rice (p. 107).

60 ml (4 tbsp) extra-virgin olive oil
450 g (1 lb) rump steak, cut into 4 serving pieces, excess fat trimmed
1.25 ml (¹/₄ tsp) black pepper
1 large onion, thinly sliced
45 ml (3 tbsp) wine vinegar
20 ml (4 tsp) Dijon mustard
60 ml (4 tbsp) home-made beef stock prepared without salt

1. In a heavy frying pan, heat 30 ml (2 tbsp) of the olive oil over moderate heat. Add steak and sauté for 2–3 minutes on each side if you would like them medium-rare and 5 minutes on each side for well done. Remove from pan using a fish slice. Sprinkle with pepper and set aside in a covered dish.

2. Add the remaining 30 ml (2 tbsp) oil to the pan and sauté onion slices for 2–3 minutes until tender. Add vinegar, mustard and stock. Stir for 2 minutes, scraping up any cooked-on bits from base of pan.

3. Pour onion sauce over steaks and serve.

Rosemary Beef Stew

This slow-cooking, wine accented stew is distinguished by the delicate taste of rosemary. Try serving it over slices of toasted bread or egg-free noodles.

450 g (1 lb) fresh tomatoes or chopped canned tomatoes
2.5 ml (¹/₂ tsp) dried basil
75 g (3 oz) chopped celery
60 ml (4 tbsp) chopped fresh parsley
1.25 ml (¹/₄ tsp) dried oregano
2.5 ml (¹/₂ tsp) dried thyme
60 ml (4 tbsp) olive oil
1.25 ml (¹/₄ tsp) black pepper
450 g (1 lb) chuck or blade steak, trimmed and cut into
  2.5-cm (1-inch) cubes
1 clove garlic, crushed
125 ml (4 fl oz) dry white wine
5 ml (1 tsp) dried rosemary

1. Combine tomatoes, basil, celery, parsley, oregano, thyme, 30 ml (2 tbsp) of the olive oil and pepper in a large saucepan. Cover and bring to the boil over high heat. Lower heat and simmer for 30 minutes.

2. While sauce is cooking heat remaining olive oil in a large heatproof casserole. Add beef and sauté for 10–15 minutes until browned. Add garlic and stir. Transfer meat to another dish, using a slotted spoon.

3. Pour wine into the casserole and cook over high heat to reduce wine by half, stirring constantly and scraping up any bits of meat in the pan. Return the meat to the pan with the rosemary and the vegetable-tomato mixture. Cover and simmer for 1¹/₂ hours or until meat is tender.

serves 4

preparation time
25 minutes

cooking time
1³/₄ hours

nutrient analysis
Calories per serving: 398
Protein: 38 gm
Carbohydrates: 9.6 gm
Dietary fibre: 1.8 gm
Cholesterol: 92 mg
Total fat: 21 gm (189 cal)
Sat fat: 4.4 gm (40 cal)
Poly fat: 1.6 gm (14 cal)
Mono fat: 12.7 gm (114 cal)

Hungarian Beef Goulash

serves 4

___

preparation time

15 minutes

___

cooking time

1 hour and 55 minutes

___

nutrient analysis

Calories per serving: 498
Protein: 39 gm
Carbohydrates: 32 gm
Dietary fibre: 2 gm
Cholesterol: 96 mg
Total fat: 23.7 gm (213 cal)
Sat fat: 5.7 gm (51 cal)
Poly fat: 1.7 gm (15 cal)
Mono fat: 14 gm (126 cal)

Goulash is a highly spiced Hungarian speciality that receives its unique flavour from the addition of paprika. Serve with a loaf of crusty French bread and some mixed greens with Citrus Dressing (p. 142).

450 g (1 lb) chuck or blade steak, cut into 2.5-cm (1-inch) cubes
60 ml (4 tbsp) olive oil
1 large onion, chopped
250 ml (8 fl oz) tomato juice
2.5 ml (¹/₂ tsp) paprika
8 small or new potatoes, scrubbed

1. Sauté steak over moderate heat in olive oil in a heavy frying pan. When meat is brown, about 10 minutes a side, add onion. Continue cooking for 5 minutes until onion is tender.
2. Add tomato juice and paprika. Cover and simmer for 1 hour. Check frequently to see if more liquid is needed, adding additional tomato juice or water as required.
3. Add potatoes and cook, covered, for 30 minutes more.

Chilli Con Carne

This traditional chilli is cooked on top of the stove. Add more chilli powder to suit your taste. Serve with a mixed green salad topped with Red Onion Dressing (p. 143) and a plate of warm tortillas or corn bread.

450 g (1 lb) lean minced beef
60 ml (4 tbsp) olive oil
1 large onion, chopped
1 green pepper, seeded and chopped
1 clove garlic, crushed
30 ml (2 tbsp) chilli powder
2.5 ml (¹/₂ tsp) ground cumin
2.5 ml (¹/₂ tsp) paprika
1 bay leaf
30 ml (2 tbsp) wine vinegar
1 litre (1³/₄ pints) water
350 g (12 oz) chopped fresh or drained canned chopped tomatoes
350 g (12 oz) cooked red kidney beans (either canned or prepared at home from dried beans)

1. Brown beef in large heavy saucepan, crumbling it with a fork until well cooked. Pour off any rendered fat and drain well. Heat olive oil in a clean pan and add browned beef, onion, green pepper and garlic. Sauté until vegetables are tender.

2. Add chilli powder, cumin paprika, bay leaf, vinegar and water. Cover and simmer for 45 minutes, stirring several times.

3. Remove bay leaf. Add tomatoes and cook for 15 minutes. Add beans and cook for an additional 15 minutes.

4. Thicken, if necessary, by mashing some of the beans with a fork or a potato masher.

Variations

* Omit the water. Add 250 ml (8 fl oz) dry white wine or light beer.
* Pour cooked chilli into an ovenproof casserole, top with grated reduced-fat cheese and bake at 180°C (350°F) mark 4 until cheese has melted.

---

serves 4

preparation time
20 minutes

cooking time
1 hour and 25 minutes

nutrient analysis
Calories per serving: 509
Protein: 44 gm
Carbohydrates: 29 gm
Dietary fibre: 8 gm
Cholesterol: 96 mg
Total fat: 24.5 gm (221 cal)
Sat fat: 5.7 gm (51 cal)
Poly fat: 1.7 gm (15 cal)
Mono fat: 14 gm (127 cal)

Hungarian Pork Chops

serves 4

___

preparation time

10 minutes

___

cooking time

1 hour and 10 minutes

___

nutrient analysis

Calories per serving: 473
Protein: 33 gm
Carbohydrates: 2 gm
Dietary fibre: 0.3 gm
Cholesterol: 108 mg
Total fat: 31 gm (281 cal)
Sat fat: 8 gm (72 cal)
Poly fat: 3.3 gm (30 cal)
Mono fat: 18 gm (161 cal)

Braise pork chops in a wine sauce that is given zest by the addition of mustard, thyme and sage. Serve with Simple Vegetable Medley (p. 97).

4 lean loin pork chops, trimmed of fat (675 g (1¹/₂ lb) with bone, before trimming)
1 small onion, chopped
60 ml (4 tbsp) olive oil
250 ml (8 fl oz) home-made chicken stock, prepared without salt, or low-salt vegetable stock
250 ml (8 fl oz) dry white wine
3.75 ml (³/₄ tsp) plain flour
5ml (1 tsp) Dijon mustard
2.5 ml (¹/₂ tsp) dried thyme
2.5 ml (¹/₂ tsp) dried sage

1. Brown pork chops and onion in olive oil in a heavy frying pan over moderate heat. When chops have browned, add stock and wine. Cover and simmer for 1 hour.

2. Slowly sprinkle flour into sauce while stirring, cooking until smooth, about 1 minute. Add mustard, thyme and sage. Heat thoroughly and serve.

Vegetable-Pork Medley

This Yugoslav dish is an unusual mixture of pork, aubergine and rice. Serve with sliced avocados and orange and grapefruit slices on Cos lettuce leaves with Nut Vinaigrette (p. 144).

450 ml (1 lb) lean pork fillet
60 ml (4 tbsp) olive oil
175 g (6 oz) thinly sliced onions
2 medium tomatoes, sliced
1.25 ml (¹/₄ tsp) black pepper
350 g (12 oz) aubergine, cubed
100 g (4 oz) green pepper, diced
225 g (8 oz) green beans, chopped
75 g (3 oz) carrots, sliced
90 g (3¹/₂ oz) raw long-grain rice
250 ml (8 fl oz) water

1. Seal pork by grilling over rack in grill pan for 3 minutes on each side. Cut pork into 2.5-cm (1-inch) pieces and set aside.

2. Preheat oven to 180°C (350°F) mark 4. Heat 5 ml (1 tbsp) of the olive oil in a medium frying pan and sauté onions for 3–5 minutes until tender.

3. Rub an ovenproof casserole with olive oil and add half the onions. Arrange half the tomato slices over onions. Sprinkle with pepper.

4. In a large bowl, combine aubergine, green pepper, beans and carrots. Add half the aubergine mixture to casserole. Add the pork and rice, then the remaining aubergine mixture. Top with the rest of the tomatoes.

5. Pour the water and remaining olive oil over casserole. Cover and bake for 1³/₄ hours or until meat and rice are tender.

serves 4

preparation time

35 minutes

cooking time

2 hours

nutrient analysis

Calories per serving: 566
Protein: 36 gm
Carbohydrates: 35 gm
Dietary fibre: 5 gm
Cholesterol: 108 mg
Total fat: 31.6 gm (284 cal)
Sat fat: 8 gm (72 cal)
Poly fat: 3.5 gm (31 cal)
Mono fat: 17.7 gm (160 cal)

Sautéed Veal Strips

serves 4

Q

preparation time

10 minutes

cooking time

6 minutes

nutrient analysis

Calories per serving: 372
Protein: 30 gm
Carbohydrates: 2 gm
Dietary fibre: 0.2 gm
Cholesterol: 116 mg
Total fat: 25.5 gm (230 cal)
Sat fat: 7.2 gm (65 cal)
Poly fat: 1.6 gm (15 cal)
Mono fat: 15 gm (137 cal)

Cut veal escalopes into thin, delicate strips before sautéeing with bay leaves, olive oil and then fresh lemon juice. Serve with Ratatouille (p. 98) and steamed rice sautéed with Basic Pesto (p. 158).

3 bay leaves
60 ml (4 tbsp) extra-virgin olive oil
450 g (1 lb) veal escalopes, cut into strips 1 cm ($^1/_2$ inch)
   wide and 7.5 cm (3 inches) long
juice of 1 lemon
1.25 ml ($^1/_4$ tsp) black pepper
45 ml (3 tbsp) chopped fresh parsley

1.   Sauté bay leaves in oil in a frying pan for 1 minute. Add veal strips and cook over high heat for 3 minutes, turning several times.

2.   Add lemon juice, pepper and parsley. Toss with veal and cook for 3–5 minutes more.

3.   Remove bay leaves and serve at once.

Veal Stew Milano

This colourful veal stew can be made a day in advance and reheated in a 180°C (350°F) mark 4 oven for 30 minutes. It can also be frozen for several months. Serve with rice and a mixed green salad with Honey-Dijon Vinaigrette (p. 144).

2 cloves garlic, crushed
2 sticks of celery, finely chopped
1 large carrot, scraped and finely chopped
1 leek, cleaned and finely chopped
1 large onion, finely chopped
125 ml (4 fl oz) olive oil
2× 397-g (14-oz) cans chopped tomatoes, drained and juice
  reserved
5 ml (1 tsp) dried basil
1.25 ml (¼ tsp) dried thyme
1.25 ml (¼ tsp) black pepper
75 g (3 oz) plain flour
900 g (2 lb) pie veal, cut into 2.5-cm (1-inch) cubes
250 ml (8 fl oz) dry white wine
300 ml (½ pint) home-made chicken stock, prepared
  without salt, or low-salt vegetable stock
30 ml (2 tbsp) finely chopped fresh parsley
15 ml (1 tbsp) grated lemon rind
15 ml (1 tbsp) grated orange rind

1. In a large frying pan, sauté garlic, celery, carrot, leek and onion in 60 ml (4 tbsp) of the olive oil for 10 minutes. Add tomatoes and half the reserved juice, the basil and thyme. Cook over moderate heat until the liquid is absorbed and sauce thickens. Transfer stew to large flameproof casserole or heavy bottomed pan.

2. Put pepper and flour into paper bag, add veal cubes, and shake until well coated. Heat remaining olive oil in frying pan and brown veal; do not crowd pieces. Place browned veal on top of vegetables in casserole.

3. Add wine to pan drippings in frying pan. Cook over high heat, and scrape up any browned bits from base. When wine is reduced by half, stir in stock and simmer for 3 minutes.

4. Pour mixture over vegetables and veal in casserole and cook on top of cooker over low heat for 1 hour or until veal is tender.

5. Sprinkle parsley and lemon and orange rind over stew immediately before serving.

serves 8

preparation time
30 minutes

cooking time
1 hour and 40 minutes

nutrient analysis

Calories per serving: 475
Protein: 35 gm
Carbohydrates: 18 gm
Dietary fibre: 1.9 gm
Cholesterol: 116 mg
Total fat: 26 gm (236 cal)
Sat fat: 7.4 gm (67 cal)
Poly fat: 1.8 gm (17 cal)
Mono fat: 15.4 gm (139 cal)

Basil-Tarragon Veal Chops

serves 4

---

preparation time

*10 minutes + 24 hours
marinating time*

---

cooking time

35 minutes

---

nutrient analysis

*Calories per serving: 398
Protein: 31 gm
Carbohydrates: 0.7 gm
Dietary fibre: 0.1 gm
Cholesterol: 116.1 mg
Total fat: 29 gm (260 cal)
Sat fat: 7.7 gm (70 cal)
Poly fat: 1.9 gm (18 cal)
Mono fat: 17.7 gm (160 cal)*

Marinate these veal chops for 24 hours before cooking them with herbs. Serve with Simple Vegetable Medley (p. 97).

*75 ml (5 tbsp) extra-virgin olive oil
2.5 ml (¹/₂ tsp) black pepper
15 ml (1 tbsp) red wine vinegar
1 clove garlic, crushed
15 ml (1 tbsp) chopped fresh parsley
30 ml (2 tbsp) finely chopped spring onions
4 lean veal loin chops, trimmed of fat (675 g (1¹/₂ lb) with
   bone before trimming)
2.5 ml (¹/₂ tsp) dried basil
2.5 ml (¹/₂ tsp) dried tarragon*

1. Combine 30 ml (2 tbsp) of the olive oil, 1.25 ml (¹/₄ tsp) of the pepper, vinegar, garlic, parsley and spring onions in a medium glass bowl.

2. Add chops, coating well with marinade. Cover bowl and refrigerate for 24 hours. Turn chops several times.

3. Remove from refrigerator and allow to return to room temperature. Preheat oven to 160°C (325°F) mark 3.

4. Brown chops in remaining oil in a large frying pan.

5. Place each chop on a 30-cm (12-inch) square of foil. Sprinkle top of each chop with half of the basil and tarragon. Turn chops over, sprinkle second side with remaining basil and tarragon. Sprinkle with remaining pepper.

6. Seal foil packages, place on a baking sheet and bake for 30 minutes until tender.

VEGETABLES

Roasted Broccoli and Cauliflower

Roasting broccoli and cauliflower at a high temperature makes their skin crispy and gives them a smoky flavour. You can also roast green beans, peppers, leeks, spring onions and onions. Roasted vegetables can be served at room temperature in salads sprinkled with vinaigrette dressing and sesame seeds or served warm, seasoned with pepper.

450 g (1 lb) broccoli florets
275 g (10 oz) cauliflower florets
60 ml (4 tbsp) extra-virgin olive oil

1. Preheat oven to 220°C (425°F) mark 7.
2. Toss vegetables and olive oil in a large bowl to completely coat them with oil and seal in their moisture.
3. Roast florets in a single layer on a baking sheet for 15 minutes. Turn the vegetables once during cooking.
4. Serve at once as a side dish or allow to cool to room temperature for salad.

serves 4

Q

preparation time

10 minutes

cooking time

15 minutes

nutrient analysis

Calories per serving: 166
Protein: 4.5 gm
Carbohydrates: 9 gm
Dietary fibre: 6.1 gm
Cholesterol: 0 mg
Total fat: 13.9 gm (125 cal)
Sat fat: 2 gm (18 cal)
Poly fat: 1.3 gm (12 cal)
Mono fat: 10 gm (90 cal)

serves 4

preparation time

15 minutes

cooking time

30 minutes

nutrient analysis

Calories per serving: 251
Protein: 2.5 gm
Carbohydrates: 22.5 gm
Dietary fibre: 5.4 gm
Cholesterol: 0 mg
Total fat: 14 gm (126 cal)
Sat fat: 2 gm (18 cal)
Poly fat: 1.3 gm (12 cal)
Mono fat: 9.7 gm (87 cal)

Carrots in Wine Sauce

Carrots, an often taken-for-granted ingredient, move centre stage when simmered in a wine sauce. Serve with Garlic Chicken (p. 67).

675 g (1¹/₂ lb) carrots, peeled and thinly sliced
1 medium onion, thinly sliced
60 ml (4 tbsp) olive oil
30 ml (2 tbsp) plain flour
175 ml (6 fl oz) dry white wine
60 ml (4 tbsp) water
15 ml (1 tbsp) finely chopped fresh parsley

1.   Steam carrots for 6–7 minutes in a vegetable steamer or cook, covered, in a microwave with a little water until crisp-tender.
2.   In a large frying pan, sauté onion in olive oil over moderate heat for 5 minutes or until softened. Stir in flour and gradually add wine and water.
3.   When sauce is smooth, add carrots and parsley. Cover loosely and simmer for 15 minutes or until carrots are done.

serves 4

preparation time

10 minutes

cooking time

30 minutes

nutrient analysis

Calories per serving: 312
Protein: 3.2 gm
Carbohydrates: 35.6 gm
Dietary fibre: 2.3 gm
Cholesterol: 0 mg
Total fat: 18 gm (165 cal)
Sat fat: 2.6 gm (23 cal)
Poly fat: 1.6 gm (14 cal)
Mono fat: 13 gm (119 cal)

Sautéed Potatoes with Red Pepper Oil

In this colourful dish, new potatoes are seasoned with chillies and red peppers. Serve with Grilled Fish Steaks (p. 74) and green beans tossed in Basic Pesto (p. 158).

675 g (1¹/₂ lb) new potatoes, scrubbed
1 clove garlic, crushed
75 ml (5 tbsp) olive oil
2.5 ml (¹/₂ tsp) crushed dried chillies
1 medium red pepper, seeded and thinly sliced
15 ml (1 tbsp) chopped spring onion

1.   In a medium saucepan, cover potatoes with water, bring to the boil and cook for 20 minutes or until tender. Drain, cool slightly and cut into quarters.
2.   Sauté garlic in olive oil over moderate heat in a large frying pan for 2 minutes. Add dried chillies and red pepper slices. Sauté for 3–5 minutes until pepper is tender.
3.   Add potatoes to pan and stir gently to heat and to coat completely with oil.
4.   Serve sprinkled with spring onions.

Simple Vegetable Medley

Steam a variety of fresh vegetables and toss with a vinaigrette sauce. Serve with Garlic Chicken (p. 67).

225 g (8 oz) broccoli florets
225 g (8 oz) cauliflower florets
175 g (6 oz) green beans, cut into 2.5-cm (1-inch) pieces
2 medium carrots, peeled and thinly sliced
1 medium red pepper, seeded and cut into 2.5-cm (1-inch) strips
50 g (2 oz) mushrooms, wiped and sliced
125 ml (4 fl oz) olive oil
30 ml (2 tbsp) red wine vinegar
30 ml (2 tbsp) chopped spring onions
1.25 ml (¹/₄ tsp) dried thyme

1. Steam broccoli, cauliflower, beans and carrots in a vegetable steamer, about 5–10 minutes, or cook covered in microwave with a little water until crisp-tender. Transfer to large serving bowl.
2. Add red pepper and mushrooms to bowl and toss to mix.
3. In a small bowl, combine oil, vinegar, spring onions and thyme. Mix with a wire whisk. Drizzle over vegetables and serve.

serves 4

Q

preparation time

15 minutes

cooking time

5–10 minutes

nutrient analysis

Calories per serving: 296
Protein: 3.7 gm
Carbohydrates: 12.4 gm
Dietary fibre: 5.2 gm
Cholesterol: 0 mg
Total fat: 27.5 gm (247 cal)
Sat fat: 3.9 gm (35 cal)
Poly fat: 2.5 gm (22.5 cal)
Mono fat: 20 gm (180 cal)

Ratatouille

serves 6

preparation time

20 minutes

cooking time

Approximately 1 hour

nutrient analysis

Calories per serving: 220
Protein: 2.3 gm
Carbohydrates: 13.7 gm
Dietary fibre: 5 gm
Cholesterol: 0 mg
Total fat: 19 gm (168 cal)
Sat fat: 2.7 gm (24 cal)
Poly fat: 1.8 gm (16 cal)
Mono fat: 13 gm (120 cal)

There are numerous approaches to making this classic dish, which originated in the south of France. The word ratatouille means poor man's stew. Make ratatouille a day ahead to allow flavours to blend, and serve it either hot, at room temperature, or cold. This simple version will keep in your refrigerator for five days.

125 ml (4 fl oz) extra-virgin olive oil
1 medium onion, finely chopped
1 clove garlic, crushed
2.5 ml (¹/₂ tsp) dried basil
2.5 ml (¹/₂ tsp) dried oregano
2.5 ml (¹/₂ tsp) dried thyme
2.5 ml (¹/₂ tsp) dried rosemary
450 g (1 lb) ripe tomatoes or 1¹/₂ × 397-g (14-oz) cans
  chopped tomatoes
1.25 ml (¹/₄ tsp) black pepper
1.25 ml (¹/₄ tsp) cayenne pepper
2 medium courgettes, sliced 5 mm (¹/₄ inch) thick
1 green pepper, seeded and thinly sliced
1 red pepper, seeded and thinly sliced
1 medium aubergine, approximately 450 g (1 lb), peeled
  and diced
30 ml (2 tbsp) finely chopped fresh parsley

1. Heat olive oil in a large, heavy saucepan. Sauté onion for 3–5 minutes until softened. Add garlic, basil, oregano, thyme and rosemary and sauté briefly.

2. Stir in tomatoes and simmer over low heat, uncovered, for 15 minutes. Add black pepper and cayenne.

3. Add courgettes, green and red peppers, aubergine and parsley to the sauce. Cover and simmer for 30 minutes. Stir once and simmer for another 10 minutes if necessary until vegetables are tender. Avoid extra stirring if possible, to retain shape of vegetables.

4. Cool and refrigerate in a glass or ceramic container overnight. Serve cold or at room temperature, garnished with lemon wedges; or reheat over low heat in a covered saucepan, stirring frequently.

Variations

★ Serve garnished with chopped spring onions, Parmesan cheese, olives or lemon wedges.

★ Omit aubergine. Use three courgettes instead of two.

Courgette Fritters

Courgette dishes are a great favourite throughout the Mediterranean region. Serve these fritters with grilled chicken or lamb chops.

2 medium courgettes
45 ml (3 tbsp) mild, light-flavoured olive oil
2 egg whites
1 clove garlic, crushed
25 g (1 oz) Parmesan cheese
1.25 ml (¹/₄ tsp) dried basil
50 g (2 oz) plain flour

1. Coarsely grate courgettes and press in a strainer to remove excess liquid.
2. Combine courgettes, 30 ml (2 tbsp) olive oil, the egg whites, garlic, cheese and basil. Stir in flour and mix well.
3. Heat remaining oil over medium heat. Drop in heaped tablespoonfuls of mixture, making 12 fritters. Flatten out each fritter slightly with the back of a spoon. Sauté until lightly browned on each side. Serve hot.

makes 12

Q

preparation time

20 minutes

cooking time

10 minutes

nutrient analysis

Calories per serving: 209
Protein: 8 gm
Carbohydrates: 15.6 gm
Dietary fibre: 2.4 gm
Cholesterol: 6.6 mg
Total fat: 12.8 gm (115 cal)
Sat fat: 3 gm (28 cal)
Poly fat: 1 gm (9 cal)
Mono fat: 8.2 gm (74 cal)

Green Bean Stew

In this colourful dish, green beans are simmered in a tomato sauce. Serve with Fish in Foil (p. 75).

450 g (1 lb) green beans, topped, tailed and cut into 2.5-cm
    (1-inch) pieces
50 g (2 oz) chopped onion
1 clove garlic, crushed
60 ml (4 tbsp) olive oil
3 medium tomatoes, chopped
30 ml (2 tbsp) finely chopped fresh parsley

1. Steam green beans for 7–10 minutes in a vegetable steamer or cook, covered, in microwave with a little water until crisp-tender.
2. Sauté onion and garlic in olive oil in a large frying pan for 5 minutes or until tender. Stir in green beans, tomatoes and parsley. Bring to the boil, then simmer 15 minutes.

serves 4

preparation time

15 minutes

cooking time

30 minutes

nutrient analysis

Calories per serving: 179
Protein: 2.9 gm
Carbohydrates: 13 gm
Dietary fibre: 3.7 gm
Cholesterol: 0 mg
Total fat: 14 gm (126 cal)
Sat fat: 2 gm (18 cal)
Poly fat: 1.4 gm (13 cal)
Mono fat: 10 gm (90 cal)

Sautéed Spinach

serves 4

Q

preparation time

15 minutes

cooking time

15 minutes

nutrient analysis

Calories per serving: 230
Protein: 9.2 gm
Carbohydrates: 9 gm
Dietary fibre: 7.1 gm
Cholesterol: 5 mg
Total fat: 19.6 gm (177 cal)
Sat fat: 3.8 gm (39 cal)
Poly fat: 1.8 gm (16 cal)
Mono fat: 13 gm (117 cal)

Steam and sauté fresh spinach in garlic-flavoured oil, then season with nutmeg and Parmesan cheese. Serve with Rump Steak with Onion-Mustard Sauce (p. 86).

900 g (2 lb) fresh spinach, well washed and trimmed
75 ml (5 tbsp) olive oil
3 cloves garlic, peeled but left whole
1.25 ml (¹/₄ tsp) ground nutmeg
1.25 ml (¹/₄ tsp) black pepper
25 g (1 oz) grated Parmesan cheese

1. Place spinach in heavy saucepan without water and cook, tightly covered, over low heat for 5 minutes or until wilted. Drain and press to remove excess liquid.

2. Heat oil in a large frying pan and add garlic. Sauté until lightly browned. Remove garlic with a slotted spoon and discard.

3. Add spinach, nutmeg and pepper to frying pan and toss in oil over moderate heat for 3–5 minutes until well coated.

4. Transfer to serving dish and sprinkle with cheese immediately before serving.

Tomato Dolma

Rice, pine nuts, dill and mint are combined in this vegetarian version of stuffed vegetables, a Turkish favourite. Serve lukewarm or cold, with Greek Lentil Soup (p. 45) and pita bread.

6 large ripe tomatoes
125 ml (4 fl oz) olive oil
1 medium onion, grated
90 g (3½ oz) raw long-grain rice
45 ml (3 tbsp) pine nuts
1.25 ml (¼ tsp) black pepper
250 ml (8 fl oz) water
5 ml (1 tsp) dried dill
5 ml (1 tsp) dried mint
30 ml (2 tbsp) finely chopped fresh parsley

1. Cut off tops of tomatoes and set aside. Carefully scoop out pulp, and turn tomatoes upside down on absorbent kitchen paper to drain. Chop pulp from 5 tomatoes (save rest for another recipe or discard).

2. Heat 60 ml (4 tbsp) of the olive oil in a large frying pan and sauté onion for 5 minutes until tender. Add rice and stir. Add pine nuts, pepper, tomato pulp and 60 ml (4 tbsp) of the water. Simmer for 5 minutes.

3. Stir in dill, mint and parsley. Preheat oven to 190° C (375° F) mark 5.

4. Half fill tomatoes with rice mixture and cover with reserved tops. Arrange in a large ovenproof casserole. Add 175 ml (6 fl oz) boiling water and the remaining olive oil. Cover and bake for 40 minutes or until stuffing is cooked.

serves 6

preparation time

20 minutes

cooking time

55 minutes

nutrient analysis

Calories per serving: 248
Protein: 2.4 gm
Carbohydrates: 19.5 gm
Dietary fibre: 2.7 gm
Cholesterol: 0 mg
Total fat: 18.5 gm (167 cal)
Sat fat: 2.6 gm (23 cal)
Poly fat: 1.8 gm (15 cal)
Mono fat: 13 gm (120 cal)

Mexican Cauliflower

serves 4

Q

preparation time

10 minutes

cooking time

25 minutes

nutrient analysis

Calories per serving: 200
Protein: 4.2 gm
Carbohydrates: 14.0 gm
Dietary fibre: 3.3 gm
Cholesterol: 1.1 mg
Total fat: 16 gm (143 cal)
Sat fat: 2.4 gm (22 cal)
Poly fat: 1.3 gm (12 cal)
Mono fat: 11 gm (98 cal)

Bake steamed cauliflower in a tomato sauce with spices and top with breadcrumbs and cheese. Serve with sautéed turkey fillets.

1 medium cauliflower, washed and separated into florets
60 ml (4 tbsp) olive oil
1 small onion, finely chopped
25 g (1 oz) chopped green pepper
227-g (8-oz) can tomatoes, chopped
15 ml (1 tbsp) chilli powder
pinch of ground cloves
15 ml (1 tbsp) ground cinnamon
1.25 ml (¹/₄ tsp) black pepper
8 stoned black olives, rinsed
30 ml (2 tbsp) fresh breadcrumbs
30 ml (2 tbsp) grated reduced-fat Cheddar cheese

1. Steam cauliflower for 5 minutes in a vegetable steamer or cook, covered, in microwave with a little water until crisp-tender.

2. Heat olive oil over moderate heat in a large frying pan. Sauté onion and green pepper for 5 minutes until tender.

3. Stir in tomatoes and cook for 3 minutes. Add chilli powder, cloves, cinnamon, black pepper and olives. Cook for 2 minutes.

4. Preheat oven to 190°C (375°F) mark 5.

5. Lightly oil a medium baking dish and place cauliflower in it. Pour tomato sauce over cauliflower.

6. Combine breadcrumbs and cheese and sprinkle over sauce. Bake for about 10 minutes until crumbs and cheese have browned.

Potato Cakes

These wonderful little treats are a combination of potatoes, cheese and onions. Serve with Split Pea Soup (p. 41).

2 medium potatoes, about 350 g (12 oz), peeled and grated
50 g (2 oz) onion, finely chopped
90 ml (6 tbsp) olive oil
25 g (1 oz) reduced-fat Cheddar cheese, grated (or other
  grated cheese such as Edam)
2 egg whites, lightly beaten
1.25 ml (¹/₄ tsp) black pepper

1. Soak grated potatoes in cold water for 5 minutes. Drain and dry on absorbent kitchen paper.
2. Sauté onion in 30 ml (2 tbsp) of the olive oil in a large frying pan for 3–5 minutes until tender.
3. Combine the sautéed onion with the potatoes, cheese, egg whites and pepper in a large bowl.
4. Heat the remaining olive oil in frying pan. Place about 45 ml (3 tbsp) of the potato mixture at a time in frying pan and use a fish slice to flatten into a small cake. Fry until brown, then turn and cook the other side. Serve hot plain, with tomato ketchup or with unsweetened apple purée.

serves 4 (2 cakes each)

Q

preparation time

20 minutes

cooking time

15 minutes

nutrient analysis

Calories per serving: 360
Protein: 11.6 gm
Carbohydrates: 23 gm
Dietary fibre: 1.5 gm
Cholesterol: 18 mg
Total fat: 25 gm (228 cal)
Sat fat: 6.4 gm (58 cal)
Poly fat: 2 gm (18 cal)
Mono fat: 16.3 gm (147 cal)

Puffed French 'Fried' Potatoes

These potatoes are a crispy, lower calorie alternative to deep-fried chips.

900 g (2 lb) potatoes
60 ml (4 tbsp) olive oil
1.25 ml (¹/₄ tsp) fresh ground pepper

1. Preheat oven to 200°C (400°F) mark 6.
2. Peel and wash potatoes. Cut potatoes lengthways in 1-cm (¹/₂-inch) slices. Cut again into strips.
3. Divide potatoes between 2 baking sheets, drizzle with olive oil, and toss to coat well. Spread out potatoes on baking sheets and sprinkle with pepper.
4. Bake for 20 minutes. Remove baking sheets from oven and allow to cool for 5 minutes.
5. Return baking sheets to oven for 10 minutes more until potatoes are lightly browned and puffed. Serve hot.

serves 4

preparation time

15 minutes

cooking time

30 minutes

nutrient analysis

Calories per serving: 315
Protein: 3.9 gm
Carbohydrates: 45.4 gm
Dietary fibre: 2.5 gm
Cholesterol: 0 mg
Total fat: 14 gm (123 cal)
Sat fat: 2 gm (18 cal)
Poly fat: 1.2 gm (11 cal)
Mono fat: 9.9 gm (90 cal)

Tabbouleh

This Near Eastern standard is a 'wheat salad', which is made from cracked bulgur wheat. Tabbouleh is a very nutritious food that tastes best when made with fresh tomatoes, parsley and mint. Syrians and Lebanese scoop up Tabbouleh with grape, lettuce or cabbage leaves as a dip. Serve with Lemon Barbecued Chicken (p. 132).

175 g (6 oz) medium-fine bulgur
350 ml (12 fl oz) cold water
60 ml (4 tbsp) extra-virgin olive oil
1 small onion, finely chopped
3 spring onions, finely chopped
2 large ripe tomatoes, chopped
8 fresh mint leaves, chopped
50 g (2 oz) fresh parsley, finely chopped
1.25 ml (¹/₄ tsp) black pepper
75 ml (5 tbsp) fresh lemon juice

1. Put bulgur wheat in a large bowl. Add water and 30 ml (2 tbsp) of the olive oil and stir. Soak for 30 minutes.

2. Line a colander with a clean tea-towel and strain bulgur wheat. Bring up sides of towel to enclose wheat and press firmly to extract as much liquid as possible. Tip bulgur wheat into serving bowl.

3. Add remaining olive oil with rest of ingredients and toss to combine well. Serve at room temperature.

Variation

Tabbouleh can be made ahead of time, chilled and served when ready. Refrigerate for 2 hours or more before serving.

serves 6

preparation time

15 minutes + 30 minutes marinating time

nutrient analysis

Calories per serving: 219.6
Protein: 2.2 gm
Carbohydrates: 12.1 gm
Dietary fibre: 1.4 gm
Cholesterol: 0 mg
Total fat: 18.8 gm (169 cal)
Sat fat: 2.6 gm (23.4 cal)
Poly fat: 1.5 gm (14.4 cal)
Mono fat: 13.2 gm (118.8 cal)

Risotto

Risotto is a special Italian rice dish with a fine, rich flavour. To make it authentic, find Italian Arborio rice in your supermarket or delicatessen. Risotto requires constant stirring, so save this recipe for a day when you're feeling patient. Present it with a cruet of olive oil. Serve with Citrus-Herb Roast Chicken (p. 69).

750 ml–1 litre (1¹/₄–1³/₄ pints) home-made chicken stock, prepared without salt, or low-salt vegetable stock
1 medium onion, chopped
90 ml (6 tbsp) extra-virgin olive oil
250 g (9 oz) raw Italian Arborio rice
25 g (1 oz) grated Parmesan cheese
1.25 ml (¹/₄ tsp) black pepper

1. In a medium saucepan, heat chicken stock to a simmer over moderate heat.

2. While stock is heating, sauté onion in olive oil in a large heatproof casserole for 3–5 minutes until soft. Add rice and stir to coat with oil.

3. Add 125 ml (4 fl oz) stock and stir with a wooden spoon until the stock has been absorbed. Continue this pattern with rest of stock, adding it 125 ml (4 fl oz) at a time and stirring until it is absorbed by the rice. When you have used all the stock, test the rice to see if it is still too chewy. If so, add more hot stock or hot water until it reaches the desired consistency.

4. Remove from heat and stir in cheese and black pepper.

serves 5

Q

preparation time

10 minutes

cooking time

Approximately 25 minutes

nutrient analysis

Calories per serving: 383
Protein: 9.2 gm
Carbohydrates: 42 gm
Dietary fibre: 0.9 gm
Cholesterol: 5.8 mg
Total fat: 19 gm (171 cal)
Sat fat: 3.8 gm (34 cal)
Poly fat: 1.6 gm (14 cal)
Mono fat: 13 gm (117 cal)

Spinach and Rice

serves 4

preparation time

15 minutes

cooking time

35 minutes

nutrient analysis

Calories per serving: 290
Protein: 4.9 gm
Carbohydrates: 23.4 gm
Dietary fibre: 3.8 gm
Cholesterol: 0 mg
Total fat: 20.8 gm (187 cal)
Sat fat: 3 gm (27 cal)
Poly fat: 1.8 gm (17 cal)
Mono fat: 15 gm (134 cal)

Serve this Greek-inspired dish with Citrus-Marinated Fish (p. 83) and fruit salad.

90 ml (6 tbsp) olive oil
1 medium onion, chopped
450 g (1 lb) fresh spinach, well washed, drained and
    chopped or 275 g (10 oz) frozen chopped spinach, thawed
90 g (3¹/₂ oz) raw long-grain rice
15 ml (1 tbsp) tomato purée
350 ml (12 fl oz) water
1.25 ml (¹/₄ tsp) black pepper
1.25 ml (¹/₄ tsp) dried dill

1. Heat olive oil in a large, heavy saucepan over moderate heat and sauté onions for 5 minutes or until lightly browned.
2. Stir in spinach, cover, and simmer for about 5 minutes or until spinach wilts.
3. Add all remaining ingredients and stir well.
4. Cover and reduce heat to low. Simmer for 25 minutes or until rice is tender.

Spanish Rice

Sauté rice, onions and green pepper in olive oil, then simmer in chicken stock and tomato sauce. Serve with Mexican Baked Fish (p. 77) and steamed green beans.

1 medium onion, finely chopped
50 g (2 oz) green pepper, finely chopped
60 ml (4 tbsp) mild light–flavoured olive oil
200 g (7 oz) long-grain rice
500 ml (17 fl oz) home-made chicken stock, prepared
*   without salt, or low-salt vegetable stock*
250 ml (8 fl oz) Basic Tomato Sauce (p. 150)
2.5 ml (¹/₂ tsp) ground cumin
1.25 ml (¹/₄ tsp) black pepper
1.25 ml (¹/₄ tsp) salt (optional)

1. Sauté onion and green pepper in olive oil over moderate heat in heavy frying pan for 5 minutes or until tender.

2. Add rice, stirring until it turns a whitish gold, about 3–5 minutes.

3. Add chicken stock, tomato sauce, cumin, black pepper and salt, if using. Bring to the boil, reduce heat to low and simmer, uncovered, for 20 minutes or until rice is done and liquid is absorbed.

serves 4

Q

preparation time

10 minutes

cooking time

25 minutes

nutrient analysis

Calories per serving: 345
Protein: 7 gm
Carbohydrates: 45.8 gm
Dietary fibre: 1.3 gm
Cholesterol: 0.5 mg
Total fat: 14.6 gm (132 cal)
Sat fat: 2.2 gm (20 cal)
Poly fat: 1.3 gm (12 cal)
Mono fat: 10.3 gm (92 cal)

Lemon-Dill Rice

This rice has a refreshing lemon-dill flavour. Serve with Sautéed Veal Strips (p. 92) and steamed marrow.

serves 4

preparation time

15 minutes

cooking time

30 minutes

nutrient analysis

Calories per serving: 342
Protein: 5.4 gm
Carbohydrates: 42 gm
Dietary fibre: 1.3 gm
Cholesterol: 0.4 mg
Total fat: 14.3 gm (129.5 cal)
Sat fat: 2.1 gm (19 cal)
Poly fat: 1.3 gm (11 cal)
Mono fat: 10 gm (92 cal)

60 ml (4 tbsp) extra-virgin olive oil
100 g (4 oz) chopped onion
200 g (7 oz) raw long-grain rice
125 ml (4 fl oz) dry white wine
grated rind of ¹/₂ lemon
350 ml (12 fl oz) home-made chicken stock. prepared
   without salt, or low-salt vegetable stock
2.5 ml (¹/₂ tsp) dried dill
1.25 ml (¹/₄ tsp) black pepper
juice of 1 lemon
30 ml (2 tbsp) chopped fresh parsley

1. Heat olive oil over moderate heat in a large frying pan and sauté onion for 5 minutes until tender. Add rice and sauté for 2 minutes.

2. Stir in wine, lemon rind, stock and dill. Cover and reduce heat to low. Simmer for 25 minutes or until rice is tender and liquid is absorbed.

3. Stir in pepper and lemon juice immediately before serving. Garnish with parsley.

New Year's Day Black-Eyed Beans

There is a tradition in the southern United States that black-eyed peas, which we perversely call black-eyed beans, must be eaten on New Year's Eve or New Year's Day for good luck. The idea was to get a dollar in the new year for each pea you ate, but with inflation that's not the same luck as it once was.

The dish, in both the hot and cold version, actually tastes best the second day and can be refrigerated for a week. Serve as a side dish with Cuban Sauce (p. 149).

225 g (8 oz) dried black-eyed beans, sorted and rinsed.
1 litre (1³/₄ pints) water
1 small onion, chopped
1 garlic clove, crushed
2.5 ml (¹/₂ tsp) black pepper
1 large bay leaf
pinch of dried thyme
30 ml (2 tbsp) wine vinegar
75 ml (5 tbsp) olive oil

1. Place black-eyed beans and water in medium saucepan and bring to the boil over high heat.

2. Reduce heat and stir in onion, garlic, pepper, bay leaf, thyme, vinegar and olive oil. Cover and simmer for 1 hour or until beans are tender. Remove bay leaf and serve black-eyed beans with rice.

Variation

For a cold salad, cook the beans and bay leaf alone in water. When tender, drain and add onion, garlic, black pepper and thyme. In a small bowl, combine vinegar and olive oil. Mix with a wire whisk. Pour over peas, stir and refrigerate at least 2 hours before serving.

serves 4

preparation time
10 minutes

cooking time
1 hour + chilling time

nutrient analysis

Calories per serving: 228
Protein: 4.9 gm
Carbohydrates: 12.5 gm
Dietary fibre: 4.1 gm
Cholesterol: 0 mg
Total fat: 18.4 gm (166 cal)
Sat fat: 2.7 gm (24 cal)
Poly fat: 1.5 gm (14 cal)
Mono fat: 13.2 gm (119 cal)

PASTA

Cooking Pasta

Cook pasta in a large saucepan of boiling water, allowing about 1 litre (1³/₄ pints) of water for every 100 g (4 oz) pasta. Slip pasta into the boiling water, a small amount at a time, so that the water keeps boiling. Stir with a fork immediately to make sure it doesn't stick together.

Fresh pasta cooks very quickly, often in 2–3 minutes; dried pasta takes between 7 and 12 minutes. Refer to individual package directions.

Taste pasta frequently to check for doneness. Stop cooking when it is al dente, tender but not mushy. Drain at once in a colander and toss with 15 ml (1 tbsp) olive oil to prevent it sticking together.

Time your sauce so that it is ready as the pasta finishes cooking to avoid the pasta becoming soft and gluey while waiting. If you are using pasta in salad, rinse it in cold water after draining.

Linguine with Oil and Garlic

Basic pasta is the best setting for a really flavourful olive oil. Serve with Broccoli Salad (p. 54) and Herb Bread (p. 166).

10 cloves garlic, crushed
125 ml (4 fl oz) extra-virgin olive oil
350 g (12 oz) linguine
1.25 ml (¹/₄ tsp) black pepper
1.25 ml (¹/₄ tsp) salt (optional)

1. Sauté garlic in 30 ml (2 tbsp) of the olive oil until lightly browned. Remove pan from heat.
2. In a large saucepan with 4 litres (7 pints) boiling water, cook linguine for 8–12 minutes or according to package directions until tender.
3. Drain in a colander and return to pan. Toss with garlic and its oil, remaining olive oil, pepper and salt, if using.

serves 4

Q

preparation time

10 minutes

cooking time

20 minutes

nutrient analysis

Calories per serving: 373
Protein: 5 gm
Carbohydrates: 28 gm
Dietary fibre: 0.7 gm
Cholesterol: 0 mg
Total fat: 28 gm (251 cal)
Sat fat: 3.8 gm (35 cal)
Poly fat: 2.3 gm (21 cal)
Mono fat: 20 gm (179 cal)

Pasta Shells with Fish Fillets and Courgette

Pair the white fish of your choice with courgette in a simmered tomato sauce and serve over pasta shells. Serve with a salad of grapefruit and orange segments, green pepper and pineapple dressed with Basic Vinaigrette (p. 144).

60 ml (4 tbsp) olive oil
30 ml (2 tbsp) chopped onion
1 clove garlic, crushed
pinch of cayenne pepper
450 g (1 lb) fresh tomatoes, chopped, or 397-g (14-oz) can chopped tomatoes, drained
5 ml (1 tsp) dried oregano
5 ml (1 tsp) dried basil
1 medium courgette, trimmed and diced
350 g (12 oz) shell pasta
350 g (12 oz) white fish fillets, cut into 2.5-cm (1-inch) pieces
30 ml (2 tbsp) chopped fresh parsley

1. Heat 45 ml (3 tbsp) of the olive oil in a large frying pan and sauté onion over moderate heat for 5 minutes or until tender. Add garlic and cayenne and sauté for 2 more minutes.
2. Add tomatoes, oregano and basil. Stir and simmer for 10 minutes.
3. Add courgette and simmer for 5 minutes more.
4. While sauce simmers, cook pasta, according to package directions, in 3 litres (7 pints) boiling water until al dente.
5. Stir fish into sauce and simmer for 5 minutes more. Drain pasta and toss with remaining olive oil. Serve sauce over shell pasta and garnish with parsley.

serves 4

preparation time

20 minutes

cooking time

25 minutes

nutrient analysis

Calories per serving: 341
Protein: 27.5 gm
Carbohydrates: 28 gm
Dietary fibre: 3.9 gm
Cholesterol: 35 mg
Total fat: 13.6 gm (123 cal)
Sat fat: 1.8 gm (17 cal)
Poly fat: 1.8 gm (17 cal)
Mono fat: 8.3 gm (75 cal)

Tuna Linguine

serves 4

Q

preparation time

10 minutes

cooking time

13 minutes

nutrient analysis

Calories per serving: 374
Protein: 17 gm
Carbohydrates: 28 gm
Dietary fibre: 0.7 gm
Cholesterol: 18.9 mg
Total fat: 22 gm (198 cal)
Sat fat: 3.2 gm (29 cal)
Poly fat: 2.1 gm (19 cal)
Mono fat: 15.2 gm (137 cal)

A speedy, delicious way to eat a serving of protein, complex carbohydrates and monounsaturates when you feel too exhausted to do much more than boil water. Serve with Israeli Salad (p. 54) and wholemeal bread.

189-g (7-oz) can tuna, preferably yellow-fin, packed in water, drained
90 ml (6 tbsp) extra-virgin olive oil
juice of 1 lemon
60 ml (4 tbsp) chopped fresh parsley
1.25 ml (¹/₄ tsp) black pepper
1.25 ml (¹/₄ tsp) salt (optional)
350 g (12 oz) linguine (or any pasta)

1. In a small bowl, break tuna into pieces and add oil. Combine with lemon juice, parsley, pepper and salt, if using.
2. Cook pasta in 4 litres (7 pints) boiling water for 8–9 minutes or according to package directions until al dente. Drain.
3. Toss with tuna sauce to combine well. Serve.

Pasta with Prawns

Season stir-fried prawns and vegetables with lemon and basil, then serve as a topping for vermicelli. Serve with wholewheat bread sticks and a bowl of peach slices.

350 g (12 oz) vermicelli
1 clove garlic, crushed
2.5 ml (¹/₂ tsp) grated lemon rind
105 ml (7 tbsp) olive oil
1 medium carrot, sliced
1 medium courgette, trimmed and thinly sliced
1 medium red pepper, seeded and cut into thin strips
450 g (1 lb) prawns, shelled and deveined
15 ml (1 tbsp) lemon juice
pinch of black pepper
5 ml (1 tsp) dried basil
15 ml (1 tbsp) finely chopped fresh parsley

1. Cook pasta according to package directions in 3 litres (7 pints) boiling water until al dente.
2. While pasta is cooking, sauté garlic and lemon rind over moderate heat in 90 ml (6 tbsp) olive oil in frying pan for 1 minute. Add carrot, courgette, red pepper and prawns. Stir-fry for 3–4 minutes.
3. Sprinkle with lemon juice, black pepper, basil and parsley.
4. Drain pasta and toss with remaining olive oil. Serve pasta with prawn and vegetable sauce on top.

serves 4

preparation time
25 minutes

cooking time
15 minutes

nutrient analysis

Calories per serving: 438
Protein: 27 gm
Carbohydrates: 25 gm
Dietary fibre: 2.4 gm
Cholesterol: 221 mg
Total fat: 25 gm (231 cal)
Sat fat: 3.7 gm (33 cal)
Poly fat: 2.6 gm (24 cal)
Mono fat: 17.6 gm (158 cal)

Pasta with Chicken and Peppers

This combination of chicken, red and green peppers and tomatoes is served with tubular pasta. Top with freshly grated Parmesan cheese. Serve with a salad of fresh or canned pears and watercress with Mint Vinaigrette (p. 144).

350 g (12 oz) tubular pasta, such as penne
75 ml (5 tbsp) olive oil
1 large boneless chicken breast, skinned and cut into strips,
    about 450 g (1 lb)
1 medium onion, chopped
1 medium red pepper, seeded and cut into thin strips
1 medium green pepper, seeded and cut into thin strips
1 clove garlic, crushed
pinch of cayenne pepper
2 large tomatoes, chopped

1. For pasta, put 3 litres (5¼ pints) water in a large saucepan over high heat.

2. While water is coming to the boil prepare sauce. Heat 30 ml (2 tbsp) of the olive oil over moderate heat in a large frying pan. Sauté chicken until it turns white. Remove chicken with a slotted spoon or tongs and set aside.

3. Add 30 ml (2 tbsp) olive oil to frying pan and sauté onion and peppers until tender.

4. Return chicken to pan and add garlic and cayenne. Cook for 3 minutes, stirring constantly.

5. Add tomatoes and simmer for 10 minutes.

6. While chicken is simmering, cook pasta, according to package instructions, until al dente. Drain and toss with remaining olive oil. Serve with chicken and peppers.

---

serves 4

preparation time

15 minutes

cooking time

25 minutes

nutrient analysis

Calories per serving: 422
Protein: 32 gm
Carbohydrates: 26 gm
Dietary fibre: 2.7 gm
Cholesterol: 75 mg
Total fat: 20 gm (188 cal)
Sat fat: 3.4 gm (30 cal)
Poly fat: 2.3 gm (21 cal)
Mono fat: 13.6 gm (123 cal)

Pasta with Spinach-Cheese Sauce

Purée wilted spinach, onion and cottage cheese to create this smooth, rich pasta sauce. Serve with sliced tomatoes and a bowl of grated Parmesan cheese.

60 ml (4 tbsp) olive oil
1 medium onion, chopped
1 clove garlic, chopped
225 g (8 oz) chopped fresh spinach, well washed and
  drained
250 ml (8 fl oz) cottage cheese
60 ml (4 tbsp) chopped fresh parsley
5 ml (1 tsp) dried basil
5 ml (1 tsp) lemon juice
1.25 ml (¹/₄ tsp) black pepper
1.25 ml (¹/₄ tsp) ground nutmeg
350 g (12 oz) spaghetti

1. Heat 45 ml (3 tbsp) of the olive oil in a large frying pan over moderate heat and sauté onion and garlic until onion is tender.

2. Add chopped spinach to pan and cook for 3–5 minutes until spinach wilts.

3. Place wilted spinach, onions and garlic in blender or food processor with cheese, parsley, basil, lemon juice, pepper and nutmeg. Blend until puréed. Leave in blender or food processor, covered, to keep sauce warm.

4. Cook pasta in 3 litres (5¹/₄ pints) boiling water, according to package directions, until al dente. Toss with remaining olive oil.

5. Add 60 ml (4 tbsp) hot water from pasta to sauce in blender and blend again. Serve over pasta.

serves 4

Q

preparation time

15 minutes

cooking time

15 minutes

nutrient analysis

Calories per serving: 274
Protein: 11.6 gm
Carbohydrates: 25 gm
Dietary fibre: 2.5 gm
Cholesterol: 2.5 mg
Total fat: 14.9 gm (134 cal)
Sat fat: 2.3 gm (21 cal)
Poly fat: 1.2 gm (11 cal)
Mono fat: 10.1 gm (91 cal)

MICROWAVE RECIPES

Olive Oil and Your Microwave

Olive oil is used mainly for flavouring in microwave cooking. We have included a wide variety of dishes that can be made in the microwave with olive oil. Try substituting olive oil for other vegetable oils in your own favourite recipes.

The recipes that follow are designed to be cooked in a 675 or 700-watt microwave oven. For ovens with an output of 650 watts or less, it may be necessary to increase the cooking times slightly. Directions indicate heat settings as 100 percent HIGH, or 50 percent MEDIUM. Rotation directions can be ignored for microwaves equipped with turntables.

---

serves 4

Q

---

preparation time

10 minutes

---

cooking time

7 minutes

---

nutrient analysis

Calories per serving: 382
Protein: 22 gm
Carbohydrates: 33.6 gm
Dietary fibre: 12.5 gm
Cholesterol: 17.9 mg
Total fat: 18.6 gm (167 cal)
Sat fat: 5.4 gm (49 cal)
Poly fat: 1.4 gm (13 cal)
Mono fat: 11.3 gm (102 cal)

Hot Bean Dip

Serve this tangy chilli-flavoured dip with crisp vegetable crudités.

675 g (1¹/₂ lb) canned kidney beans, drained with 75 ml
   (5 tbsp) reserved liquid
60 ml (4 tbsp) olive oil
100 g (4 oz) reduced-fat Cheddar cheese, grated
15 ml (1 tbsp) finely chopped onion
15 ml (1 tbsp) chilli powder
1.25 ml (¹/₄ tsp) paprika

1. Combine beans, olive oil and reserved 75 ml (5 tbsp) bean liquid in a 2 litre (3¹/₂ pint) microwave-safe bowl. Cover with microwave-safe cling film. Heat at 100 percent HIGH for 4 minutes.

2. Remove from oven and mash bean mixture with fork or potato masher until smooth.

3. Stir in cheese, onion, chilli powder and paprika. Cover again and microwave at 100 percent HIGH for approximately 3 minutes or until cheese melts.

4. Remove from microwave and serve warm.

Aubergine Salad Spread

Serve this smooth and tangy spread with savoury biscuits or pita bread wedges.

1 large aubergine
50 g (2 oz) chopped onion
50 g (2 oz) finely chopped celery
1 clove garlic, crushed
5 ml (1 tsp) dried oregano
1.25 ml (¹/₄ tsp) black pepper
60 ml (4 tbsp) extra-virgin olive oil
30 ml (2 tbsp) wine vinegar
30 ml (2 tbsp) pine nuts (optional)

1. Place aubergine on paper plate, prick with a fork and cook, uncovered, at 100 percent HIGH for 12 minutes. Remove and cool.
2. Cut aubergine in half and scoop out pulp, placing it in a blender or food processor.
3. Add onion, celery, garlic, oregano and pepper and process at medium speed until well blended.
4. Place in a medium bowl and stir in olive oil and wine vinegar. Sprinkle with pine nuts.
5. Cover and chill for several hours, stirring occasionally. Serve chilled or at room temperature.

serves 4

preparation time

10 minutes + several hours chilling time

cooking time

12 minutes

nutrient analysis

Calories per serving: 173
Protein: 1.4 gm
Carbohydrates: 9.8 gm
Dietary fibre: 3.2 gm
Cholesterol: 0 mg
Total fat: 15.4 gm (139 cal)
Sat fat: 2 gm (19 cal)
Poly fat: 1.7 gm (15 cal)
Mono fat: 11 gm (99 cal)

Chicken with Green Peppers

serves 4

Q

preparation time

10 minutes

cooking time

12 minutes

nutrient analysis

Calories per serving: 350
Protein: 37 gm
Carbohydrates: 10.3 gm
Dietary fibre: 3.3 gm
Cholesterol: 94 mg
Total fat: 17.9 gm (161 cal)
Sat fat: 3.2 gm (29 cal)
Poly fat: 2.2 gm (20 cal)
Mono fat: 11.5 gm (103 cal)

Chicken and green peppers are cooked with tomatoes, onions and olive oil in this easy to prepare recipe. Serve with Baked New Potatoes with Paprika (p. 129).

60 ml (4 tbsp) mild light-flavoured olive oil
1 large onion, chopped
2 medium green peppers, seeded and cut into strips
4 large tomatoes, cut into quarters
1.25 ml (¼ tsp) black pepper
2 boneless chicken breasts, 450 g (1 lb), skinned and cut in half to make 4 pieces

1. Heat oil in an uncovered microwave-safe baking dish for 2 minutes at 100 percent HIGH. Add onion, cover with microwave-safe cling film, and cook for 2 minutes more at 100 percent HIGH.

2. Take baking dish out of microwave. Put green peppers, tomatoes and black pepper in a bowl. Pour oil-onion mixture over vegetables and stir to coat.

3. Return vegetables to the centre of the baking dish. Surround with the 4 chicken pieces. Cover tightly and cook at 100 percent HIGH for 10 minutes.

4. Remove from microwave. Uncover carefully and check to make sure chicken is done. Return to microwave for 1–2 minutes more to complete cooking, if necessary.

Crumbed Turkey Breasts

Turkey breasts are coated in breadcrumbs and cooked in the microwave in this simple recipe. Serve with Quick Microwave Tomato Sauce (p. 124) and Spinach with Oil and Garlic (p. 127).

4 turkey breasts, 450 g (1 lb), cut in half
30 ml (2 tbsp) mild, light-flavoured olive oil
2 egg whites, slightly beaten
75 g (3 oz) dried breadcrumbs (or half breadcrumbs and
  half oat bran)
25 g (1 oz) grated Parmesan cheese
pinch of black pepper
500 g (17 oz) Quick Microwave Tomato Sauce (p. 124)

1. Pound turkey breast halves between two pieces of greaseproof paper until they are 5 mm (¹/₄ inch) thick.

2. Beat olive oil into egg whites in a shallow dish or soup plate.

3. Combine breadcrumbs, Parmesan cheese and pepper in a second shallow dish.

4. Dip each turkey breast into oil-egg mixture and then into crumb mixture. Place in 1 layer on microwave-safe baking dish. Cover tightly with microwave-safe cling film and cook at 100 percent HIGH for 6 minutes.

5. Rotate dish and rearrange turkey pieces so all sides cook. Cook for 5 minutes more.

6. Remove from oven. Uncover carefully and check that turkey is done. Return to microwave for 1–2 minutes more, if necessary to complete cooking.

serves 4

Q

preparation time

10 minutes

cooking time

12 minutes

nutrient analysis

Calories per serving: 480
Protein: 33 gm
Carbohydrates: 21.6 gm
Dietary fibre: 0.4 gm
Cholesterol: 64 mg
Total fat: 26.4 gm (238 cal)
Sat fat: 5.2 gm (47 cal)
Poly fat: 2.6 gm (23 cal)
Mono fat: 16 gm (144 cal)

Fish Steaks in Vegetable Sauce

serves 4

preparation time

15 minutes

cooking time

25 minutes

nutrient analysis

Calories per serving: 342
Protein: 31.8 gm
Carbohydrates: 9 gm
Dietary fibre: 2.8 gm
Cholesterol: 47 mg
Total fat: 17 gm (155 cal)
Sat fat: 2.5 gm (22 cal)
Poly fat: 2.4 gm (21 cal)
Mono fat: 11 gm (99 cal)

Use your microwave to steam the vegetables and poach the fish in this tasty dish. Serve with pasta.

60 ml (4 tbsp) extra-virgin olive oil
1 clove garlic, crushed
1 medium onion, finely chopped
2 small courgettes, chopped
1 small carrot, scrubbed and finely chopped
175 g (6 oz) fresh tomatoes, chopped, or drained canned
   tomatoes
125 ml (4 fl oz) dry white wine
5 ml (1 tsp) dried dill
1.25 ml (¼ tsp) salt (optional)
4 fish steaks, 450 g (1 lb), about 2 cm (¾ inch) thick

1.   Place olive oil in a 2-litre (3½-pint), microwave-safe bowl. Add garlic and onion, cover with microwave-safe cling film, and cook for 2 minutes at 100 percent HIGH.

2.   Add courgettes, carrot, tomatoes, wine, dill, and salt, if using. Cover and cook at 100 percent HIGH for 10 minutes, stirring several times.

3.   Place fish in vegetable sauce with thicker sides pointing toward the outside edges of the bowl. Cook at 100 percent HIGH for 10 minutes, without covering. Rotate dish half-way through cooking time and rearrange fish so all sides cook evenly. Fish is done when it flakes easily when tested with a fork and is no longer translucent.

Baked Pork Loin Chops

Bake lean pork loin chops in an herb-tomato sauce. Serve with Potato Cubes and Broccoli (p. 128).

4 × 1 cm (¹/₂ inch) thick pork loin chops, trimmed of fat
60 ml (4 tbsp) mild light-flavoured olive oil
2 cloves garlic, chopped
1.25 ml (¹/₄ tsp) dried oregano
1.25 ml (¹/₄ tsp) dried basil
1.25 ml (¹/₄ tsp) black pepper
1 green pepper, seeded and diced
100 g (4 oz) fresh tomatoes, chopped or drained canned
*   tomatoes*

1. Place pork chops in a large microwave-safe baking dish with the fleshy parts of the chop pointing towards the outsides of the dish. Cover with microwave-safe cling film and cook at 100 percent HIGH for 14 minutes. Turn chops over and rearrange after 7 minutes. Rotate dish several times while cooking. Remove from microwave. Cut into pork chops near the bone to make sure there are no pink juices. Return and microwave for 2 minutes more if not completely cooked. When done, remove from microwave and set aside.

2. Combine oil and garlic in a 2 litre (3¹/₂ pint) microwave-safe dish. Cook at 100 percent HIGH for 45 seconds. Add oregano, basil, black pepper, green pepper and tomatoes. Cook for 5 minutes, stirring several times. Remove from oven.

3. Pour sauce over pork chops in baking dish and cover with microwave-safe cling film. Microwave at 100 percent HIGH for 3 minutes.

serves 4

Q

preparation time

10 minutes

cooking time

25 minutes

nutrient analysis

Calories per serving: 425
Protein: 32.3 gm
Carbohydrates: 3.6 gm
Dietary fibre: 0.6 gm
Cholesterol: 108 mg
Total fat: 31 gm (280 cal)
Sat fat: 7.9 gm (71 cal)
Poly fat: 3.3 gm (30 cal)
Mono fat: 17.7 gm (160 cal)

Stuffed Peppers

Stuff red peppers with a mixture of minced turkey, rice, tomatoes, onion and basil. Serve with Spinach with Oil and Garlic (p. 127).

serves 4

Q

preparation time

15 minutes

cooking time

30 minutes

nutrient analysis

Calories per serving: 263
Protein: 4 gm
Carbohydrates: 31.7 gm
Dietary fibre: 2.6 gm
Cholesterol: 0 mg
Total fat: 14.4 gm (130 cal)
Sat fat: 2.4 gm (22 cal)
Poly fat: 1.8 gm (16 cal)
Mono fat: 10.3 gm (92 cal)

4 medium red peppers
60 ml (4 tbsp) mild, light-flavoured olive oil
1 medium onion, finely chopped
175 g (6 oz) minced turkey
397-g (14-oz) can chopped tomatoes, drained
90 g (3¹/₂ oz) raw long-grain rice
2.5 ml (¹/₂ tsp) salt (optional)
5 ml (1 tsp) dried basil
1.25 ml (¹/₄ tsp) black pepper
125 ml (4 fl oz) water
30 ml (2 tbsp) tomato purée

1. Cut tops off of peppers and reserve. Carefully scoop out pepper cores and seeds, keeping shells intact.

2. Heat olive oil in a large microwave-safe dish, uncovered, for 2 minutes at 100 percent HIGH. Add onion and turkey. Stir. Cook for 5 minutes, uncovered, at 100 percent HIGH.

3. Add tomatoes, rice, salt, if using, basil and black pepper and mix well.

4. Stuff cored peppers with turkey mixture and put tops back on peppers. Arrange stuffed peppers in a microwave-safe baking dish.

5. Combine water and tomato purée. Pour over and around peppers and tightly cover baking dish. Microwave at 100 percent HIGH for 20 minutes. Remove from oven, uncover and allow to stand for 5 minutes.

Aubergine with Tomatoes and Penne

Microwave aubergine in an olive-tomato sauce and serve with tubular pasta. Garnish with grated Parmesan cheese. Serve a salad of endive, chicory, baby tomatoes and cucumber slices topped with Red Onion Dressing (p. 143).

60 ml (4 tbsp) extra-virgin olive oil
2 cloves garlic, crushed
2×397-g (14-oz) cans chopped tomatoes
30 ml (2 tbsp) chopped black olives
2.5 ml (¹/₂ tsp) dried oregano
1.25 ml (¹/₄ tsp) black pepper
2.5 ml (¹/₂ tsp) salt (optional)
1 medium aubergine, peeled and diced
350 g (12 oz) penne or other tubular pasta

1. Heat olive oil and garlic in a 2 litre (3¹/₂ pint) microwave-safe dish at 100 percent HIGH for 1 minute.
2. Add tomatoes, olives, oregano, pepper and salt, if using, and mix well. Microwave at 100 percent HIGH, uncovered, for 3 minutes. Stir several times.
3. Add aubergine and stir to coat with tomato mixture. Cover and cook at 100 percent HIGH for 3 minutes. Stir several times.
4. Cook penne, according to package directions, in 3 litres (5³/₄ pints) of water until al dente. Drain and toss with 15 ml (1 tbsp) olive oil. Serve with aubergine-tomato sauce.

serves 4

Q

preparation time

10 minutes

cooking time

7 minutes

nutrient analysis

Calories per serving: 225
Protein: 4.6 gm
Carbohydrates: 21.7 gm
Dietary fibre: 4.2 gm
Cholesterol: 0 mg
Total fat: 15.5 gm (14 cal)
Sat fat: 2.1 gm (19 cal)
Poly fat: 1.5 gm (14 cal)
Mono fat: 10.7 gm (97 cal)

Quick Microwave Tomato Sauce

makes 1 litre (1³/₄ pints)

Q

preparation time

9 minutes

cooking time

20 minutes

nutrient analysis

Calories per serving: 176
Protein: 1.5 gm
Carbohydrates: 7.4 gm
Dietary fibre: 1.2 gm
Cholesterol: 0 mg
Total fat: 13.9 gm (125 cal)
Sat fat: 2 gm (18 cal)
Poly fat: 1.3 gm (12 cal)
Mono fat: 10 gm (90 cal)

This all-purpose sauce can be served 'as is' or may be used as a base for a meat sauce with the addition of lean minced beef or turkey.

60 ml (4 tbsp) extra-virgin olive oil
1 clove garlic, crushed
1 small onion, chopped
60 ml (4 tbsp) dry white wine
397-g (14-oz) can chopped tomatoes
15 ml (1 tbsp) tomato purée
1.25 ml (¹/₄ tsp) black pepper
1.25 ml (¹/₄ tsp) salt (optional)
5 ml (1 tsp) dried basil

1. Combine oil, garlic and onion in a 3-litre (5¹/₄-pint) microwave-safe bowl. Cover with microwave-safe film and cook for 2 minutes at 100 percent HIGH.
2. Add wine, tomatoes, tomato purée, pepper, salt, if using, and basil. Cover and cook at 100 percent HIGH for 5 minutes. Uncover and cook at 50 percent MEDIUM for 15 minutes. Allow to stand for 7 minutes before serving.

Cauliflower and Green Beans Vinaigrette

Toss fresh cauliflower and green beans in an oil and vinegar dressing and serve at room temperature. Serve with Tuna Linguine (p. 112).

225 g (8 oz) cauliflower florets
125 ml (4 fl oz) water
225 g (8 oz) green beans, topped, tailed and cut into 2.5-cm (1-inch) pieces
60 ml (4 tbsp) olive oil
30 ml (2 tbsp) wine vinegar
1.25 ml (¹/₄ tsp) salt (optional)
1.25 ml (¹/₄ tsp) black pepper

1. Place cauliflower florets in a single layer in a microwave-safe baking dish with 60 ml (4 tbsp) water. Cover with microwave-safe cling film. Cook at 100 percent HIGH for 4 minutes. Allow to stand for 3 minutes.

2. Place beans in a microwave-safe baking dish with 60 ml (4 tbsp) water. Cover and cook at 100 percent HIGH for 6 minutes, stirring once. Allow to stand for 2 minutes.

3. Drain cauliflower and beans and toss together in a salad bowl.

4. Shake oil, vinegar, salt, if using, and pepper in a small jar or mix with a wire whisk to combine well. Pour over vegetables and serve.

serves 4

Q

preparation time

15 minutes

cooking time

10 minutes

nutrient analysis

Calories per serving: 153
Protein: 2.2 gm
Carbohydrates: 7.5 gm
Dietary fibre: 2.6 gm
Cholesterol: 0 mg
Total fat: 13.8 gm (124 cal)
Sat fat: 2 gm (18 cal)
Poly fat: 1.2 gm (11 cal)
Mono fat: 10 gm (90 cal)

Tri-Coloured Pepper Bake

serves 4

Q

preparation time

15 minutes

cooking time

8 minutes

nutrient analysis

Calories per serving: 151
Protein: 1.2 gm
Carbohydrates: 6.9 gm
Dietary fibre: 1.8 gm
Cholesterol: 0 mg
Total fat: 14 gm (26 cal)
Sat fat: 2 gm (18 cal)
Poly fat: 1.4 gm (13 cal)
Mono fat: 10 gm (90 cal)

Bake red, green and yellow peppers in an olive oil sauce. Serve with Crumbed Turkey Breasts (p. 119).

3 medium red peppers, seeded and cut into strips
1 medium yellow pepper, seeded and cut into strips
2 medium green peppers, seeded and cut into strips
60 ml (4 tbsp) mild, light-flavoured olive oil
1 clove garlic, crushed
2.5 ml (¹/₂ tsp) dried oregano
1.25 ml (¹/₄ tsp) salt (optional)
pinch of black pepper
60 ml (4 tbsp) chopped fresh parsley

1. Place red pepper strips on the base of a 2-litre (3¹/₂-pint) microwave-safe dish. Top with yellow and green pepper strips.

2. Combine olive oil, garlic, oregano, salt, if using, and black pepper. Mix with a wire whisk. Pour over peppers. Tightly cover dish with microwave-safe cling film. Microwave at 100 percent HIGH for 6–8 minutes.

3. Remove from oven and carefully pierce film with knife tip to release steam. Remove cling film with care. Garnish bake with parsley before serving.

Mushrooms in Oil-Garlic Sauce

Microwave mushrooms in oil and garlic, then sprinkle with parsley. Serve hot, sprinkled with Parmesan cheese, or at room temperature as part of canapés.

60 ml (4 tbsp) olive oil
2 cloves garlic, crushed
450 g (1 lb) mushrooms, wiped and thinly sliced
45 ml (3 tbsp) finely chopped fresh parsley
1.25 ml (¹/₄ tsp) salt (optional)
1.25 ml (¹/₄ tsp) black pepper

1. Place oil and garlic in a 2-litre (3¹/₂-pint) microwave-safe bowl. Cover with microwave-safe cling film and cook at 100 percent HIGH for 2 minutes.
2. Stir in mushrooms. Re-cover and cook at 100 percent HIGH for 5 minutes, stirring twice.
3. Remove from microwave and sprinkle with parsley, salt, if using, and pepper.

serves 4

Q

preparation time

15 minutes

cooking time

8 minutes

nutrient analysis

Calories per serving: 152
Protein: 2.5 gm
Carbohydrates: 6 gm
Dietary fibre: 2.2 gm
Cholesterol: 0 mg
Total fat: 14 gm (126 cal)
Sat fat: 2 gm (18 cal)
Poly fat: 1.3 gm (12 cal)
Mono fat: 10 gm (90 cal)

Spinach with Oil and Garlic

Use this cooking method with other leafy vegetables.

60 ml (4 tbsp) olive oil
2 cloves garlic, crushed
575 g (1¹/₄ oz) frozen spinach
1.25 ml (¹/₄ tsp) salt (optional)
1.25 ml (¹/₄ tsp) black pepper

1. Combine olive oil and garlic in a 4-litre (7-pint) microwave-safe casserole. Cook for 1 minute.
2. Add frozen spinach. Cover with microwave-safe cling film and cook at 100 percent HIGH for 10 minutes, stirring several times. Add salt, if using, and pepper and serve.

serves 4

Q

preparation time

5 minutes

cooking time

11 minutes

nutrient analysis

Calories per serving: 161
Protein: 4.6 gm
Carbohydrates: 8.1 gm
Dietary fibre: 3.0 gm
Cholesterol: 0 mg
Total fat: 13.8 gm (124 cal)
Sat fat: 1.9 gm (18 cal)
Poly fat: 1.3 gm (11 cal)
Mono fat: 10 gm (90 cal)

Potato Cubes and Broccoli

serves 5

Q

preparation time

20 minutes

cooking time

15 minutes

nutrient analysis

Calories per serving: 271
Protein: 5.4 gm
Carbohydrates: 35 gm
Dietary fibre: 5.6 gm
Cholesterol: 0 mg
Total fat: 14 gm (126 cal)
Sat fat: 2 gm (18 cal)
Poly fat: 1.3 gm (12 cal)
Mono fat: 10 gm (90 cal)

Toss potatoes and broccoli with onion and celery in a garlic-oil sauce. Serve with microwave baked plaice fillets.

675 g (1¹/₂ lb) potatoes, peeled and cut into 2.5-cm (1-inch) cubes
75 ml (5 tbsp) water
450 g (1 lb) broccoli, cut into 2.5-cm (1-inch) florets
75 ml (5 tbsp) olive oil
1 clove garlic, chopped
60 ml (4 tbsp) wine vinegar
1.25 ml (¹/₄ tsp) black pepper
1.25 ml (¹/₄ tsp) salt (optional)
50 g (2 oz) celery, thinly sliced
50 g (2 oz) onion, chopped

1. Combine potatoes and water in 3-litre (5¹/₄-pint) microwave-safe casserole. Cover with microwave-safe cling film and cook at 100 percent HIGH for 10 minutes. Stir once.
2. Layer broccoli on top of potatoes in casserole. Re-cover. Microwave at 100 percent HIGH for 3 minutes. Remove casserole and drain vegetables.
3. Place oil and garlic in the empty casserole, cover, and return to microwave. Microwave at 100 percent HIGH for 1¹/₂ minutes. Remove from microwave and stir in vinegar, pepper, salt, if using, potatoes, broccoli, celery and red onion. Serve at once.

Baked New Potatoes with Paprika

Bake new potatoes with garlic, oil and paprika. Serve with a salad, meat or minced turkey loaf, and fresh green beans steamed in the microwave.

12 small new potatoes, scrubbed
5 cloves garlic, chopped
60 ml (4 tbsp) mild, light-flavoured olive oil
1.25 ml (¼ tsp) paprika
1.25 ml (¼ tsp) salt (optional)

1. Place potatoes, garlic, olive oil, paprika and salt, if using, in a 2-litre (3½-pint) microwave-safe dish. Toss potatoes to coat well with oil mixture. Tightly cover dish.
2. Microwave at 100 percent HIGH for 10 minutes if potatoes are small, 15 if they are large. Rearrange potatoes in dish once during cooking period.
3. Remove from oven. Uncover and serve.

serves 4

Q

preparation time

10 minutes

cooking time

15 minutes

nutrient analysis

Calories per serving: 299
Protein: 3.7 gm
Carbohydrates: 41.8 gm
Dietary fibre: 3.4 gm
Cholesterol: 0 mg
Total fat: 13.8 gm (124 cal)
Sat fat: 2 gm (18 cal)
Poly fat: 1.2 gm (11 cal)
Mono fat: 10 gm (90 cal)

Lemon Scalloped Potatoes

Microwave sliced potatoes in a lemon-oil sauce and season with lemon rind, Parmesan cheese and oregano. Serve with microwaved boneless chicken breasts and green salad with Parsley-Spring Onion Vinaigrette (p. 145).

3 large potatoes, scrubbed and thinly sliced
60 ml (4 tbsp) mild, light-flavoured olive oil
15 ml (1 tbsp) lemon juice
10 ml (2 tsp) grated lemon rind
45 ml (3 tbsp) grated Parmesan cheese
2.5 ml (½ tsp) dried oregano
1.25 ml (¼ tsp) salt (optional)

1. Arrange potato slices in a large microwave-safe baking dish. Sprinkle with olive oil and lemon juice.
2. Combine lemon rind, Parmesan cheese, oregano and salt, if using. Sprinkle over potatoes.
3. Tightly cover dish with microwave-safe cling film. Cook at 100 percent HIGH for 12 minutes. Remove from oven and carefully remove film.
4. Return to oven and cook uncovered at 100 percent HIGH for 5 minutes.

serves 4

Q

preparation time

15 minutes

cooking time

15 minutes

nutrient analysis

Calories per serving: 229
Protein: 3.7 gm
Carbohydrates: 21 gm
Dietary fibre: 1.1 gm
Cholesterol: 3.7 mg
Total fat: 15 gm (135 cal)
Sat fat: 2.8 gm (26 cal)
Poly fat: 1.2 gm (11 cal)
Mono fat: 10.3 gm (93 cal)

FROM THE BARBECUE

Barbecue Tips

Warm weather cooking often finds us standing in front of our barbecues, where olive oil is an ideal ingredient for all of our favourite dishes.

In recent years, the pleasure of outdoor cooking has been clouded by reports that burnt meats may create carcinogens. When the fat in meat drips on to the coals, the combustion causes potentially harmful smoke to rise and be absorbed on the surface of the meat. To make barbecuing safe, you can take a few simple preventative measures.

1. First, cook foods at lower temperatures. This will require raising your barbecue grill further above the heat source.

2. If you use wood when you barbecue, use hardwoods and avoid soft woods such as pine.

3. Do not use pine cones as fuel.

4. Keep fat from dripping on to your heat source and producing smoke. Put a metal drip pan or piece of heavy duty foil in the centre of your bed of charcoal underneath your barbecuing food. Keep coals to one side and food to the other.

Proper circulation, which is very important, is easier to obtain with a kettle-style barbecue than with a small hibachi. Barbecue in a well-ventilated location where any smoke that does form can drift away instead of accumulating on your food. Also experiment with using foil on your grill as we do in some of the following recipes to prevent food from coming into contact with the flame.

In keeping with your low cholesterol diet guidelines, don't overemphasize red meat in your barbecue menus. Fish is a good choice since it appears to form few mutagens and also contains fats that may protect against cancer.

When you do barbecue meat, use lower-fat cuts of beef so that fat doesn't drip on coals and cause flareups. To further reduce fat content, precook the meat in a microwave at 100 percent HIGH for 30 seconds–1^1/$_2$ minutes before cooking and discard any juice that collects. Don't eat liquid drippings and cut away any charred portions.

Don't barbecue frozen meat since the outside chars while the inside remains frozen.

You may also wish to consider barbecuing over a gas grill because these are more convenient to use and do not require the use of charcoal or wood products. They also provide even heat, which is helpful when you are cooking for longer time periods at lower temperatures. Neither gas nor electric barbecues are thought to be significantly safer than charcoal barbecues since chemicals form when fat drips on any heat source. However, the Swedes have invented a vertical grill, which is reported to be very effective in reducing the risks from chemicals.

Most barbecued foods are also delicious if cooked in advance and served at room temperature or slightly chilled. They are also excellent in salads.

Poultry

Poultry generally requires a longer, slower cooking time than meat or fish on the barbecue. If possible, cook on a covered barbecue using moderate heat and baste frequently. Chicken pieces require about 15 minutes on each side, while chicken and turkey breasts need about 8 minutes a side.

Fish

Moderately fat (with healthful omega-3 oils), full-flavoured fish, such as salmon, trout and mackerel, are suggested for barbecuing as opposed to more delicately flavoured fish such as sole. Avoid over-cooking fish so as not to change its texture and taste. It is done when it flakes when tested with a fork.

Shellfish

Prawns and scallops are also simple to barbecue and can be prepared with a wide variety of marinades to provide interesting flavours.

Lemon-Barbecued Chicken

serves 4

preparation time

15 minutes

cooking time

35–45 minutes

nutrient analysis

Calories per serving: 429
Protein: 35 gm
Carbohydrates: 2.3 gm
Dietary fibre: 0.05 gm
Cholesterol: 94 mg
Total fat: 30 gm (278 cal)
Sat fat: 5 gm (45 cal)
Poly fat: 3.2 gm (29 cal)
Mono fat: 21 gm (192 cal)

Baste chicken with a lemon and olive oil sauce flavoured with brown sugar, dry mustard, thyme, rosemary and tarragon. Serve with Ratatouille (p. 98) and crusty French rolls.

125 ml (4 fl oz) extra-virgin olive oil
60 ml (4 tbsp) lemon juice
125 ml (4 fl oz) water
5 ml (1 tsp) brown sugar
5 ml (1 tsp) mustard powder
1.25 ml (¹/₄ tsp) dried thyme
1.25 ml (¹/₄ tsp) dried rosemary
1.25 ml (¹/₄ tsp) dried tarragon
*2 whole chicken breasts, total weight 450 g (1 lb), cut in
    half, rinsed and patted dry*

1. For barbecue sauce, combine olive oil, lemon juice, water, brown sugar, mustard, thyme, rosemary and tarragon in a small saucepan. Heat to boiling point, lower heat, and keep warm.

2. Brush chicken with barbecue sauce. Place chicken over moderate heat on grill and barbecue slowly, turning frequently for 35–45 minutes. Begin to baste with barbecue sauce after chicken browns and continue doing so until chicken is cooked.

Turkey Breasts in Citrus Marinade

Turkey breasts are quick and easy to barbecue. For a change of pace, marinate them in this citrus sauce. Serve with Green Bean Salad (p. 61) and baked potatoes in foil.

125 ml (4 fl oz) orange juice
30 ml (2 tbsp) light soy sauce
5 ml (1 tsp) chopped fresh root ginger
2 cloves garlic, crushed
1 small onion, finely chopped
5 ml (1 tsp) honey
5 ml (1 tsp) Dijon mustard
60 ml (4 tbsp) extra-virgin olive oil
450 g (1 lb) turkey breasts, 1 cm (¹/₂ inch) thick

1. Combine orange juice, soy sauce, root ginger, garlic, onion, honey, mustard and olive oil in a large glass bowl.
2. Marinate turkey breasts in olive oil mixture for 2 hours in refrigerator.
3. Barbecue over moderate heat for 3–5 minutes per side until done to your taste.
4. Bring remaining marinade to the boil, pour over turkey breasts and serve.

serves 4

preparation time

15 minutes + 2 hours marinating time

cooking time

6–10 minutes

nutrient analysis

Calories per serving: 333
Protein: 35 gm
Carbohydrates: 7.2 gm
Dietary fibre: 0.6 gm
Cholesterol: 79 mg
Total fat: 17.6 gm (158 cal)
Sat fat: 3.1 gm (28 cal)
Poly fat: 2.1 gm (19 cal)
Mono fat: 10.7 gm (94 cal)

Barbecued Fish in a Basket

serves 4

---

preparation time

25 minutes

---

cooking time

15 minutes

---

nutrient analysis

Calories per serving: 359
Protein: 45 gm
Carbohydrates: 0.7 gm
Dietary fibre: 0.02 gm
Cholesterol: 70 mg
Total fat: 18 gm (166 cal)
Sat fat: 2.2 gm (20 cal)
Poly fat: 2.7 gm (24 cal)
Mono fat: 11.6 gm (104 cal)

Since fish fall apart easily and can be difficult to turn when barbecuing, a good solution is to split the fish lengthways and barbecue it open faced in a wire basket grill. Try this method, which produces a crispy-skinned fish, with trout or salmon. Serve with sweetcorn roasted in foil and grilled tomatoes with Basic Pesto (p. 158).

60 ml (4 tbsp) olive oil
675 g (1¹/₂ lb) whole fish, cleaned, head and tail removed
30 ml (2 tbsp) lemon juice
1.25 ml (¹/₄ tsp) dried thyme
1.25 ml (¹/₄ tsp) dried rosemary
1.25 ml (¹/₄ tsp) black pepper

1. Rub a folding wire basket grill with a little olive oil. Split the fish and place it in the grill.
2. In a small glass bowl, combine olive oil, lemon juice, thyme, rosemary and pepper.
3. Brush fish with olive oil mixture. Cook for approximately 15 minutes over moderate heat, turning frequently and basting with the olive oil mixture several times. Remove from heat when done to your taste.
4. When removing fish from basket grill, place grill over a plate. Loosen fish from the wires on the top half of the grill. Open grill and carefully turn it over on to a serving platter. Gently loosen any fish sticking to basket grill wires.

Foil-Wrapped Whole Fish

An alternative method of barbecuing whole fish is to wrap them in foil. In this recipe, whole fresh fish is wrapped in foil with olive oil, onions and a medley of herbs. The result is moist and full of flavour. Serve with barbecued whole onions and baked potatoes in foil. Use finely chopped herbs if available.

60 ml (4 tbsp) olive oil
1 medium onion, sliced
675 g (1 lb) fish, cleaned, head and tail removed
1.25 ml (¼ tsp) black pepper
2.5 ml (½ tsp) chopped fresh parsley
1.25 ml (¼ tsp) dried tarragon
1.25 ml (¼ tsp) dried dill
1.25 ml (¼ tsp) dried thyme
1.25 ml (¼ tsp) dried rosemary

1. Pour half the olive oil in the centre of a large piece of heavy-duty foil. Sprinkle half the sliced onions over the olive oil.
2. Place fish on top of onion slices.
3. Pour the rest of the onion slices and olive oil over fish. Sprinkle with herbs.
4. Bring foil around fish, sealing top and ends with a double fold.
5. Place on barbecue over moderate heat. Cook for 25 minutes, turning foil package several times. Serve fish with juices spooned over each serving.

serves 4

Q

preparation time

10 minutes

cooking time

25 minutes

nutrient analysis

Calories per serving: 367
Protein: 46 gm
Carbohydrates: 2.2 gm
Dietary fibre: 0.5 gm
Cholesterol: 70 mg
Total fat: 18.6 gm (167 cal)
Sat fat: 2.6 gm (23 cal)
Poly fat: 2.8 gm (25 cal)
Mono fat: 11.6 gm (104 cal)

Barbecued Scallops

Scallops have a special flavour after being marinated in olive oil and lime juice and then barbecued. Serve with potato slices and dill baked in foil and skewered mushrooms, green peppers and baby tomatoes.

30 ml (2 tbsp) finely chopped spring onions
1 clove garlic, crushed
30 ml (2 tbsp) fresh lime juice
60 ml (4 tbsp) extra-virgin olive oil
1.25 ml ($^1/_4$ tsp) black pepper
450 g (1 lb) scallops

1.   Combine spring onions, garlic, lime juice, olive oil and black pepper in a large glass bowl.
2.   Add scallops to bowl and marinate for 30 minutes.
3.   Thread scallops on 4 skewers and cook over moderate heat for 8 minutes or until done to your taste. Turn several times during cooking and baste with remaining marinade.

Variation

Marinate scallops in a ginger-honey marinade. Combine 45 ml (3 tbsp) lemon juice, 60 ml (4 tbsp) olive oil, 15 ml (1 tbsp) honey, 15 ml (1 tbsp) soy sauce and 1 clove garlic, crushed. Marinate for 3 hours in the refrigerator before barbecuing. Dip scallops in 25 g (1 oz) toasted sesame seeds before serving.

serves 4

preparation time

10 minutes + 30 minutes marinating time

cooking time

Approximately 8 minutes

nutrient analysis

Calories per serving: 249
Protein: 26 gm
Carbohydrates: 3 gm
Dietary fibre: 0.04 gm
Cholesterol: 60 mg
Total fat: 15 gm (135 cal)
Sat fat: 1.9 gm (17 cal)
Poly fat: 1.4 gm (12 cal)
Mono fat: 9.9 gm (89 cal)

Zesty Barbecued Fish

A third method of barbecuing fish, in addition to foil wrapping and cooking in a basket grill, works well for fillets. Try this with firm mackerel, trout or bass. This spicy barbecue sauce also works well with chicken. Serve with barbecued aubergine and barbecued fresh pineapple slices.

125 ml (4 fl oz) olive oil
60 ml (4 tbsp) wine vinegar
2.5 ml (¹/₂ tsp) mustard powder
5 ml (1 tsp) brown sugar
350 ml (12 fl oz) water
5 ml (1 tsp) chilli powder
1.25 ml (¹/₄ tsp) Tabasco sauce
1.25 ml (¹/₄ tsp) black pepper
2.5 ml (¹/₂ tsp) paprika
¹/₂ clove garlic, crushed
¹/₂ medium onion, finely chopped
1.25 ml (¹/₄ tsp) cayenne pepper
4 fish fillets, about 450 g (1 1lb)

1. Combine olive oil, vinegar, mustard, brown sugar, water, chilli powder, Tabasco sauce, black pepper, paprika, garlic, onion and cayenne in a large saucepan. Bring to the boil and cook for 10 minutes.
2. Transfer the saucepan to the side of your barbecue grill. Thread each fish fillet over a long fork, piercing it in two places to hold it securely.
3. Dip the fillets in the sauce and barbecue over moderate heat. Baste the fish with the sauce every 2 minutes and cook until done. Carefully remove from barbecue with a wide spatula and serve with remaining sauce.

serves 4

Q

preparation time

10 minutes

cooking time

10–15 minutes

nutrient analysis

Calories per serving: 402
Protein: 30 gm
Carbohydrates: 2.7 gm
Dietary fibre: 0.4 gm
Cholesterol: 46.7 mg
Total fat: 30 gm (270 cal)
Sat fat: 4.3 gm (38 cal)
Poly fat: 3.4 gm (30 cal)
Mono fat: 21 gm (189 cal)

Shish Kebab

serves 4

preparation time

*15 minutes + 3 hours
marinating time*

cooking time

10 minutes

nutrient analysis

*Calories per serving: 519
Protein: 50 gm
Carbohydrates: 10 gm
Dietary fibre: 2.3 gm
Cholesterol: 167 mg
Total fat: 31 gm (286 cal)
Sat fat: 9.4 gm (85 cal)
Poly fat: 2.3 gm (20.9 cal)
Mono fat: 16.4 gm (147 cal)*

Marinated, skewered lamb dishes appear in many cuisines from the lamb brochettes of Provence to the shish kebab of Turkey. This version can be cooked over an outdoor barbecue or grilled in your oven. Serve with Lemon-Dill Rice (p. 108).

675 g (1½ lb) boneless lamb shoulder or leg, cut into
    2.5-cm (1-inch) cubes
1 onion, cut into quarters
2 green peppers, seeded and cut into 2.5-cm (1-inch) pieces
2 tomatoes, cut into quarters
60 ml (4 tbsp) olive oil
75 ml (5 tbsp) lemon juice
5 ml (1 tsp) black pepper
2 cloves garlic, crushed
2.5 ml (½ tsp) dried thyme
2.5 ml (½ tsp) dried oregano

1. Place meat, onion, peppers and tomatoes in a medium glass bowl.
2. Make marinade by combining olive oil, lemon juice, pepper, garlic, thyme and oregano in a small bowl. Pour over lamb and vegetables. Cover and marinate for 3 hours in a cool place.
3. Thread meat and vegetables on skewers, alternating meat with vegetables. Barbecue over moderate heat, basting with remaining marinade, for 12 minutes or until cooked to your liking.

Spanish Kebabs
Omit marinade. Use 60 ml (4 tbsp) olive oil; 1 small onion, chopped; 2 cloves garlic, crushed; 30 ml (1 tbsp) finely chopped fresh parsley; 5 ml (1 tsp) paprika; 1.25 ml (¼ tsp) cayenne pepper; 1.25 ml (¼ tsp) dried oregano; and 1.25 ml (¼ tsp) ground cumin.

Teriyaki Kebabs
Marinate 450 g (1 lb) lean sirloin steak, cut in strips 5 mm (¼ inch) thick and 2.5 cm (1 inch) wide, in 125 ml (4 fl oz) light soy sauce, 5 ml (1 tsp) brown sugar, 60 ml (4 tbsp) olive oil, 15 ml (1 tbsp) finely chopped root ginger, 1.25 ml (¼ tsp) black pepper and 2 cloves garlic, crushed, in a glass bowl for 2 hours in the refrigerator. Thread steak strips on 4 skewers, accordian style. Place a water chestnut on the end of each skewer. Barbecue over moderate heat

for 12 minutes or until done, turning often and basting with marinade.

Lamb Aubergine Kebabs

Marinate 675 g (1¹/₂ lb) of lean lamb leg or shoulder, trimmed and cut in 2.5-cm (1-inch) cubes in 125 ml (4 fl oz) olive oil, 75 ml (5 tbsp) lemon juice, 1 clove garlic, crushed, 5 ml (1 tsp) dried rosemary, 5 ml (1 tsp) dried thyme and 1.25 ml (¹/₄ tsp) black pepper in a glass bowl overnight in the refrigerator. When ready to cook, peel the aubergine and cut it into 2.5-cm (1-inch) pieces. Alternately thread lamb and aubergine cubes on to skewers. Brush with leftover marinade and barbecue over moderate heat for 10 minutes. Brush with marinade and cook for 10 more minutes or until lamb is cooked to your liking.

Fish Kebabs

Marinate 450 g (1 lb) firm, meaty fish steaks or fillets, cut in 2.5-cm (1-inch) pieces in 125 ml (4 fl oz) olive oil, 60 ml (4 tbsp) wine vinegar, 1 clove garlic, crushed, and 1.25 ml (¹/₄ tsp) dried oregano in a glass bowl in the refrigerator for 30 minutes. Thread fish chunks on skewers alternating with 1 large onion, cut in 2.5-cm (1-inch) cubes; 1 medium green pepper, seeded and cut in 2.5-cm (1-inch) pieces; 12 baby tomatoes; and 1 small courgette, cut in 2.5-cm (1-inch) slices. Cook kebabs for approximately 5 minutes on each side, basting with remaining marinade.

Mixed Vegetable Kebabs

Steam 1 medium courgette, cut in 2-cm (³/₄-inch) slices and 1 medium butternut squash cut in 2-cm (³/₄-inch) slices for 3 minutes. Steam 8 small onions for 10 minutes. Cool onions and peel. Add 1 small aubergine, cut in 2-cm (³/₄-inch) slices; 1 medium red pepper, seeded and cut in 8 pieces; and 8 large mushrooms. Marinate in 15 ml (1 tbsp) lemon juice, 15 ml (1 tbsp) wine vinegar, 1 clove garlic, crushed, 5 ml (1 tsp) dried basil, 1.25 ml (¹/₄ tsp) dried thyme, 15 ml (1 tbsp) chopped fresh parsley, 5 ml (1 tsp) Dijon mustard, 60 ml (4 tbsp) olive oil, and 1.25 ml (¹/₄ tsp) black pepper in a glass bowl for 4 hours in the refrigerator. Stir frequently. Thread vegetables alternately on 4 skewers and barbecue over moderate heat for 10 minutes on each side or until done to suit your taste. Baste frequently with remaining marinade.

Vegetable-French Bread Kebabs

Soak 1 loaf of French bread, cut in 2.5-cm (1-inch) cubes in 125 ml (4 fl oz) olive oil. Alternately thread barbecue skewers with a cube of bread, a large fresh mushroom, a 2.5-cm (1-inch) cube of low-fat cheese, a cube of bread, a baby tomato, a cube of cheese, a cube of bread, a 2.5-cm (1-inch) square piece of green pepper, a cube of cheese, and a final cube of bread. Barbecue skewers over moderate heat for 10 minutes until bread is toasted and cheese melts. Eat at once.

Barbecued Potatoes and Pesto

serves 4

Q

preparation time

10 minutes

cooking time

20 minutes

nutrient analysis

Calories per serving: 272
Protein: 3.6 gm
Carbohydrates: 34.1 gm
Dietary fibre: 1.9 gm
Cholesterol: 1.2 mg
Total fat: 14 gm (127 cal)
Sat fat: 2.3 gm (21 cal)
Poly fat: 1.2 gm (11 cal)
Mono fat: 10 gm (90 cal)

Barbecue potatoes with Parmesan cheese and the pesto of your choice in foil packages. Serve with barbecued turkey burgers and Dill and Lentil Salad (p. 59).

675 g (1¹/₂ lb) potatoes, scrubbed and cut in half
60 ml (4 tbsp) pesto (any from p. 158)
15 ml (1 tbsp) grated Parmesan cheese

1. Boil potatoes in a large pan of water for 10 minutes over moderate heat. Drain and cool.

2. Cut 4×25-cm (10-inch) pieces of heavy-duty foil. Place a quarter of the potatoes on each piece of foil. Spoon 15 ml (1 tbsp) pesto on each potato package. Sprinkle with Parmesan cheese and wrap securely.

3. Barbecue foil packages over moderate heat for 10 minutes.

Barbecued Garlic Bread

Traditional garlic bread tastes better than ever when prepared on the barbecue. Serve with a platter of ripe tomato slices and cubes of low-fat cheese.

1 medium-sized loaf French bread, cut into 1-cm (¹/₂-inch)
slices
2 cloves garlic, cut in half
60 ml (4 tbsp) olive oil
1.25 ml (¹/₄ tsp) black pepper

1. Toast the bread slices on the barbecue grill over moderate heat until the marks from the grill appear on the surface of the bread.
2. Remove from grill and rub while hot with halved garlic cloves.
3. Drizzle with olive oil, sprinkle with pepper and serve.

serves 4 (3 slices each)

Q

preparation time

5 minutes

nutrient analysis

Calories per serving: 278
Protein: 0.1 gm
Carbohydrates: 32 gm
Dietary fibre: 0 gm
Cholesterol: 0 mg
Total fat: 14 gm (126 cal)
Sat fat: 1.9 gm (17 cal)
Poly fat: 1.3 gm (12 cal)
Mono fat: 10 gm (90 cal)

ON THE SIDE

Citrus Dressing

This tangy dressing spiced with ginger works well with fruit or poultry salads.

75 ml (5 tbsp) orange juice
15 ml (1 tbsp) lemon juice
10 ml (2 tsp) finely chopped, peeled fresh root ginger
3 spring onions, thinly sliced
30 ml (2 tbsp) wine vinegar
1.25 ml (¹/₄ tsp) black pepper
125 ml (4 fl oz) mild, light-flavoured olive oil

1. In a medium bowl, mix orange juice, lemon juice, root ginger, spring onions, vinegar and pepper with a fork or wire whisk.
2. Slowly add oil, whisking until dressing has thickened. Serve at room temperature.

Variation
Omit ginger. Add 15 ml (1 tbsp) finely chopped fresh dill and pour over potato salad.

serves 8 (30 ml/2 tbsp each)

Q

preparation time

10 minutes

nutrient analysis

Calories per serving: 132
Protein: 0.23 gm
Carbohydrates: 4.1 gm
Dietary fibre: 0.2 gm
Cholesterol: 0 mg
Total fat: 13.5 gm (122 cal)
Sat fat: 1.9 gm (17 cal)
Poly fat: 1.1 gm (9.9 cal)
Mono fat: 9.3 gm (84 cal)

Parsley Dressing

This smooth, tangy dressing can be used on green salads, poultry, fish or seafood salads.

50 g (2 oz) parsley leaves
25 g (1 oz) chives cut into 2.5-cm (1-inch) pieces
1 clove garlic
30 ml (2 tbsp) Dijon mustard
175 ml (6 fl oz) extra-virgin olive oil
60 ml (4 tbsp) wine vinegar
45 ml (3 tbsp) lemon juice
1.25 ml (¹/₄ tsp) black pepper

1. Purée the parsley, chives and garlic in a blender or food processor.
2. Add mustard, olive oil, vinegar, lemon juice and black pepper. Blend until smooth.

serves 14 (30 ml/2 tbsp each)

Q

preparation time

10 minutes

nutrient analysis

Calories per serving: 107
Protein: 0.3 gm
Carbohydrates: 1.4 gm
Dietary fibre: 0.4 gm
Cholesterol: 0 mg
Total fat: 11.7 gm (104 cal)
Sat fat: 1.7 gm (15 cal)
Poly fat: 1 gm (9 cal)
Mono fat: 9 gm (81 cal)

Red Onion Dressing

Mild red onions, wine vinegar and mustard powder give this dressing a zesty flavour that works particularly well with mixed salads.

250 ml (8 fl oz) extra-virgin olive oil
60 ml (4 tbsp) lemon juice
60 ml (4 tbsp) wine vinegar
2.5 ml (¹/₂ tsp) mustard powder
5 ml (1 tsp) finely chopped red onion
2.5 ml (¹/₂ tsp) dried oregano
2.5 ml (¹/₂ tsp) dried thyme
2 cloves garlic, crushed

1. Combine all ingredients in a tightly covered jar and shake energetically until ingredients are well blended.
2. Store at room temperature for 2–3 hours before using.

serves 12 (30 ml/2 tbsp each)

Q

preparation time

10 minutes

nutrient analysis

Calories per serving: 161
Protein: 0.1 gm
Carbohydrates: 1 gm
Dietary fibre: 0 gm
Cholesterol: 0 mg
Total fat: 18 gm (162 cal)
Sat fat: 2.6 gm (23 cal)
Poly fat: 1.5 gm (14 cal)
Mono fat: 13.3 gm (120 cal)

Basic Vinaigrette

serves 10 (30 ml/2 tbsp each)

Q

preparation time

10 minutes

nutrient analysis

Calories per serving: 191
Protein: 0 gm
Carbohydrates: 0.5 gm
Dietary fibre: 0 gm
Cholesterol: 0 mg
Total fat: 22 gm (190 cal)
Sat fat: 3.1 gm (28 cal)
Poly fat: 1.8 gm (16 cal)
Mono fat: 15.9 gm (143 cal)

Basic vinaigrette dressing can be adapted to highlight a wide variety of salad recipes and provide a unique menu accent. Try serving Cumin Vinaigrette with a meal with a Mexican flavour or Sesame Vinaigrette when you're serving Oriental dishes.

75 ml (5 tbsp) wine or cider vinegar
1.25 ml (¹/₄ tsp) salt (optional)
1.25 ml (¹/₄ tsp) black pepper
250 ml (8 fl oz) extra-virgin olive oil

1. Mix vinegar, salt, if using, and pepper with a fork or wire whisk.
2. Slowly whisk in oil until well blended.

Variations

* ★ Herb Vinaigrette: Add 5 ml (1 tsp) each of mustard powder, basil, tarragon.
* ★ Anchovy Vinaigrette: Add 50 g (2 oz) anchovy fillets, chopped.
* ★ Avocado Vinaigrette: Add ¹/₂ small avocado, mashed and 2.5 ml (¹/₂ tsp) Worcestershire sauce.
* ★ Balsamic Vinaigrette: Omit wine vinegar. Use balsamic vinegar. Add 15 ml (1 tbsp) of finely chopped shallots and 1.25 ml (¹/₄ tsp) dried marjoram.
* ★ Chive Vinaigrette: Add 10 ml (2 tsp) finely chopped fresh chives.
* ★ Creamy Dijon Vinaigrette: Add 10 ml (2 tsp) Dijon mustard and 7.5 ml (1¹/₂ tsp) mayonnaise.
* ★ Cumin Vinaigrette: Add 2.5 ml (¹/₂ tsp) ground cumin.
* ★ Curry Vinaigrette: Add 10 ml (2 tsp) curry powder and 15 ml (1 tbsp) finely chopped spring onions.
* ★ Dijon Vinaigrette: Add 10 ml (2 tsp) Dijon mustard.
* ★ Honey-Dijon Vinaigrette: Add 15 ml (1 tbsp) Dijon mustard and 30 ml (2 tbsp) honey.
* ★ Mint Vinaigrette: Add 30 ml (2 tbsp) chopped fresh mint.
* ★ Olive Vinaigrette: Add 40 g (1¹/₂ oz) chopped black or green olives.
* ★ Orange Vinaigrette: Add 10 ml (2 tsp) grated orange rind and 45 ml (3 tbsp) fresh orange juice.
* ★ Nut Vinaigrette: Add 25 g (1 oz) finely chopped almonds or walnuts.
* ★ Parmesan Vinaigrette: Add 15 ml (1 tbsp) grated Parmesan cheese.

* Parsley-Spring Onion Vinaigrette: Add 15 ml (1 tbsp) chopped fresh parsley and 1 finely chopped spring onion.
* Gherkin Vinaigrette: Add 15 ml (1 tbsp) finely chopped fresh parsley, 30 ml (2 tbsp) finely chopped gherkin, 15 ml (1 tbsp) finely chopped green pepper and 5 ml (1 tsp) grated onion.
* Raspberry Vinaigrette: Omit wine vinegar. Use raspberry vinegar.
* Rosy Vinaigrette: Add 15 ml (1 tbsp) tomato ketchup, 1.25 ml ($^1/_4$ tsp) dried tarragon, 1.25 ml ($^1/_4$ tsp) mustard powder, 1.25 ml ($^1/_4$ tsp) paprika.
* Sesame Vinaigrette: Add 2 cloves crushed garlic and 30 ml (2 tbsp) toasted sesame seeds.

Tomato Dressing

This quick and easy blender dressing is made from fresh tomatoes. Try it with a salad of Cos lettuce, spring onions and cucumbers.

3 medium ripe fresh tomatoes
60 ml (4 tbsp) olive oil
1 clove garlic, crushed
1.25 ml ($^1/_4$ tsp) cayenne pepper

1. Cut tomatoes into quarters.
2. Place tomatoes, olive oil, garlic and cayenne in a blender container. Blend until smooth.

serves 6–8

Q

preparation time

10 minutes

nutrient analysis

Calories per serving: 55
Protein: 0.3 gm
Carbohydrates: 1.7 gm
Dietary fibre: 0.6 gm
Cholesterol: 0 mg
Total fat: 5.5 gm (50 cal)
Sat fat: 0.8 gm (7 cal)
Poly fat: 0.5 gm (4 cal)
Mono fat: 4 gm (36 cal)

One Egg Blender Mayonnaise

serves 8 (30 ml/2 tbsp each)

Q

preparation time

10 minutes

---

nutrient analysis

Calories per serving: 190
Protein: 0.8 gm
Carbohydrates: 0.16 gm
Dietary fibre: 0.0 gm
Cholesterol: 34 mg
Total fat: 21 gm (189 cal)
Sat fat: 3.1 gm (28 cal)
Poly fat: 1.8 gm (16 cal)
Mono fat: 15 gm (135 cal)

Although it isn't possible to make authentic mayonnaise without egg yolks, this version reduces the cholesterol by only using one yolk. Remember to include the yolk in your weekly allowance!

15 ml (1 tbsp) Dijon mustard (or 2.5 ml/½ tsp dry
    mustard plus 5 ml/1 tsp wine vinegar)
5 ml (1 tsp) lemon juice
1 egg
175 ml (6 fl oz) mild, light flavoured olive oil

1. Mix mustard, lemon juice and egg yolk in a blender or food processor. Allow to stand for 3 minutes.
2. Switch on the blender or processor again and add olive oil slowly in a very thin stream through the hole in the cap or the feeder tube. When all the oil has been added, push down around edges with a rubber spatula.
3. Refrigerate for 1 hour before serving.

Variation

Omit Dijon mustard. Use 1.25 ml (¼ tsp) mustard powder, 1 crushed garlic clove and 1.25 ml (¼ tsp) black pepper.

Note

Due to some recent concerns about salmonella food poisoning from raw eggs, it is recommended that dried pasteurised eggs be used in this recipe, especially for consumption by the elderly, the very young, pregnant women and people of poor health.

Sauces

One of the easiest and quickest ways to add olive oil to your diet is by using sauces and marinades that include it. Although many of the recipes in other chapters incorporate sauces, we have added a collection of sauces and marinades for you to mix and match with your favourite foods. For the best taste, use extra-virgin olive oil.

Chilli Barbecue Sauce

This spicy sauce comes from Mexico. Use as a basting sauce for barbecuing or roasting meat and poultry.

125 ml (4 fl oz) extra-virgin olive oil
1 medium onion, chopped
1 clove garlic, crushed
1 small fresh chilli, finely chopped
30 ml (2 tbsp) chilli powder
2 large ripe tomatoes, chopped
60 ml (4 tbsp) wine vinegar
60 ml (4 tbsp) water
2.5 ml (¹/₂ tsp) salt (optional)

1. Heat 15 ml (1 tbsp) olive oil in a frying pan. Sauté onions for 5 minutes until softened.
2. Add garlic, chilli, chilli powder and tomatoes and simmer until sauce starts to thicken.
3. Add vinegar, water and salt, if using. Cook for 8 minutes, stirring constantly. Use immediately or refrigerate for later use.

serves 8 (60 ml/4 tbsp each)

Q

preparation time

10 minutes

cooking time

15 minutes

nutrient analysis

Calories per serving: 136
Protein: 0.7 gm
Carbohydrates: 3.6 gm
Dietary fibre: 0.6 gm
Cholesterol: 0 mg
Total fat: 14 gm (124 cal)
Sat fat: 1.9 gm (17 cal)
Poly fat: 1.2 gm (11 cal)
Mono fat: 10 gm (90 cal)

serves 9 (60 ml/4 tbsp each)

preparation time

10 minutes

cooking time

30 minutes

nutrient analysis

Calories per serving: 236
Protein: 0.1 gm
Carbohydrates: 1.1 gm
Dietary fibre: 0.07 gm
Cholesterol: 0 mg
Total fat: 24 gm (216 cal)
Sat fat: 3.4 gm (31 cal)
Poly fat: 2.03 gm (18 cal)
Mono fat: 17.7 gm (159 cal)

Wine Basting Sauce

This sauce can be adapted for use with fish, poultry or meat by varying the type of wine and choice of herbs.

2 cloves garlic, crushed
250 ml (8 fl oz) dry white wine or red wine
60 ml (4 tbsp) lemon juice
250 ml (8 fl oz) olive oil
5 ml (1 tsp) black pepper
5 ml (1 tsp) dried thyme, basil or oregano

1.   Simmer all ingredients over low heat for 30 minutes in a small covered saucepan.
2.   Use warm or cold sauce to baste fish, meat or poultry. Can be refrigerated up to 1 week.

serves 4 (125 ml/4 fl oz each)

Q

preparation time

10 minutes

cooking time

20 minutes

nutrient analysis

Calories per serving: 144
Protein: 1.6 gm
Carbohydrates: 5.5 gm
Dietary fibre: 2 gm
Cholesterol: 0 mg
Total fat: 13.8 gm (124 cal)
Sat fat: 2 gm (18 cal)
Poly fat: 1.2 gm (11 cal)
Mono fat: 10 gm (90 cal)

Cayenne Sauce

This sauce is made with canned tomatoes and can be served with pasta or vegetables.

60 ml (4 tbsp) olive oil
2×213-g (7¹/₂-oz) cans plum tomatoes, drained and
   chopped
1 clove garlic, crushed
2.5 ml (¹/₂ tsp) dried tarragon
pinch of cayenne pepper
20 ml (4 tsp) fresh parsley, finely chopped
1.25 ml (¹/₄ tsp) black pepper.

1.   Heat oil in a medium (non-aluminium) saucepan over moderate heat.
2.   Add all remaining ingredients. Cover and simmer over low heat for 20 minutes, stirring occasionally with a wooden spoon.

Cuban Sauce

This sauce is traditionally eaten with black beans, and it also tastes wonderful with meat, poultry or seafood.

4 medium red peppers, quartered, seeded and cored
60 ml (4 tbsp) olive oil
2 garlic cloves, crushed
¹/₂×213-g (7¹/₂-oz) can plum tomatoes, drained and
  chopped
1.25 ml (¹/₄ tsp) sugar
1.25 ml (¹/₄ tsp) black pepper
pinch of cayenne pepper
1.25 ml (¹/₄ tsp) dried oregano
15 ml (1 tbsp) red wine vinegar

1. Preheat grill. Put peppers on a baking sheet and rub well with some olive oil (reserve remaining oil).
2. Place peppers under grill, 7.5 cm (3 inches) from heat, turning frequently until all sides are blackened and charred.
3. Allow peppers to cool. Peel with a sharp paring knife.
4. Process peppers in a blender or food processor with garlic and tomatoes until smooth. Add sugar, black pepper, cayenne and oregano.
5. Simmer in a saucepan over low heat, adding remaining olive oil. Simmer for 20 minutes or until thickened, stirring occasionally with a wooden spoon.
6. Pour in vinegar immediately before serving. Eat warm or at room temperature.

serves 4

Q

preparation time

10 minutes

cooking time

20 minutes

nutrient analysis

Calories per serving: 151.9
Protein: 1.2 gm
Carbohydrates: 7.6 gm
Dietary fibre: 1.8 gm
Cholesterol: 0 mg
Total fat: 14 gm (126 cal)
Sat fat: 2 gm (18 cal)
Poly fat: 1.4 gm (13 cal)
Mono fat: 10 gm (90 cal)

Basic Tomato Sauce

serves 5 (250ml/8 fl oz each)

Use this all-purpose sauce on pasta, meat, fish or vegetable dishes.

preparation time

10 minutes

cooking time

1 hour

nutrient analysis

Calories per serving: 200
Protein: 3.7 gm
Carbohydrates: 18 gm
Dietary fibre: 1.6 gm
Cholesterol: 0 mg
Total fat: 14 gm (130 cal)
Sat fat: 2 gm (19 cal)
Poly fat: 1.4 gm (13 cal)
Mono fat: 10 gm (90 cal)

100 g (4 oz) onion, chopped
1 clove garlic, crushed,
75 ml (5 tbsp) olive oil
60 ml (4 tbsp) chopped fresh parsley
30 ml (2 tbsp) chopped fresh basil (or 15 ml (1 tbsp) dried basil)
175 g (6 oz) tomato purée
397-g (14-oz) can chopped tomatoes
2.5 ml (¹/₂ tsp) sugar
pinch of salt
pinch of black pepper

1. Sauté onion and garlic in oil in a heavy (non-aluminium) saucepan for 3 minutes.

2. Add all remaining ingredients and stir with a wooden spoon.

3. Bring sauce to the boil and reduce heat to low. Simmer for 1 hour, stirring occasionally. Use immediately or refrigerate and use as needed.

Variations

* Use fresh tomatoes. Fry 1 large onion, finely chopped, in 60 ml (4 tbsp) olive oil. Add 1.4 kg (3 lb) tomatoes, skinned and chopped. Stir in 1.25 ml (¹/₄ tsp) each of black pepper and sugar, plus 5 ml (1 tsp) dried oregano and 15 ml (1 tbsp) dried basil. Simmer for 45 minutes. If not using immediately, pour into jar and cover with 5 mm (¹/₄ inch) layer of olive oil. Will keep in refrigerator for up to 1 week.
* For a hotter sauce, add fresh grated horseradish to taste. Serve with shellfish.

Greek Oil and Lemon Sauce

This versatile sauce can be used instead of mayonnaise over grilled or poached fish, poured over salads, and as a dressing for steamed vegetables. It can also be used to baste fish that is being barbecued or cooked under a grill.

125 ml (4 fl oz) extra-virgin olive oil
30 ml (2 tbsp) lemon juice
1.25 ml (¹/₄ tsp) black pepper
15 ml (1 tbsp) chopped fresh parsley

1. Process oil, lemon juice and pepper in a blender or food processor.
2. Add parsley and process until well blended.

serves 4 (30 ml/2 tbsp each)

Q

preparation time
10 minutes

nutrient analysis

Calories per serving: 241
Protein: 0.07 gm
Carbohydrates: 0.8 gm
Dietary fibre: 0.09 gm
Cholesterol: 0 mg
Total fat: 27 gm (243 cal)
Sat fat: 3.8 gm (34 cal)
Poly fat: 2.3 gm (20 cal)
Mono fat: 20 gm (180 cal)

Spicy Tomato Sauce with Wine

Try serving this all-purpose tomato sauce as a topping for baked jacket potatoes.

60 ml (4 tbsp) olive oil
30 ml (2 tbsp) finely chopped onion
1 clove garlic, crushed
3 medium ripe tomatoes, chopped
15 ml (1 tbsp) tomato purée
125 ml (4 fl oz) dry white wine
30 ml (2 tbsp) water
15 ml (1 tbsp) finely chopped fresh parsley
1.25 ml (¹/₄ tsp) cayenne pepper
dash of Tabasco sauce
1 bay leaf
pinch of salt
1.25 ml (¹/₄ tsp) black pepper

1. Heat oil in a frying pan and fry onion and garlic for 3–5 minutes until softened. Add tomatoes and stir-fry for 2 minutes more.
2. Add remaining ingredients and stir. Cover and simmer for 30 minutes. Strain sauce before serving.

serves 4 (125 ml/4 fl oz each)

preparation time
20 minutes

cooking time
35 minutes

nutrient analysis

Calories per serving: 144
Protein: 1.1 gm
Carbohydrates: 5.6 gm
Dietary fibre: 1.7 gm
Cholesterol: 0 mg
Total fat: 14 gm (124 cal)
Sat fat: 2 gm (18 cal)
Poly fat: 1.2 gm (11 cal)
Mono fat: 10 gm (90 cal)

Marinades

Marinades can be mixed with a wooden spoon, shaken in a jar, or mixed in a blender or food processor. They can be prepared fresh or in advance and stored in a jar in the refrigerator, overnight or longer.

Wash, wipe and dry foods before marinating; do not marinate frozen foods since they will dilute the marinade as they thaw. Place foods to be marinated in glass, ceramic, enamel or stainless steel containers. Avoid plastic, cast-iron, aluminium or copper containers.

Foods to be marinated for less than an hour can be left at room temperature in a covered container. For longer marinating times, cover and store foods in the refrigerator. While delicate fish may require only an hour to marinate, tough meat may require as much as two days.

If food is not completely immersed in marinade, remember to turn it several times. Marinating tenderises food and may consequently reduce cooking time by as much as one third.

serves 4 (60 ml/4 tbsp each)

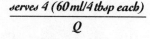

preparation time

10 minutes

nutrient analysis

Calories per serving: 360
Protein: 0 gm
Carbohydrates: 0.9 gm
Dietary fibre: 0.03 gm
Cholesterol: 0 mg
Total fat: 40.5 gm (365 cal)
Sat fat: 5.8 gm (52 cal)
Poly fat: 3.5 gm (31 cal)
Mono fat: 30 gm (0.27 cal)

Basic Marinade

Use this herb marinade for marinating and basting chicken, fish or meat.

30 ml (2 tbsp) wine vinegar
1 clove garlic, crushed
15 ml (1 tbsp) Dijon mustard
1.25 ml (¹/₄ tsp) dried parsley
1.25 ml (¹/₄ tsp) dried thyme
1.25 ml (¹/₄ tsp) dried marjoram
175 ml (6 fl oz) olive oil
1.25 ml (¹/₄ tsp) black pepper

1. In a small bowl, mix vinegar with garlic, mustard, parsley, thyme and marjoram.
2. Whisk in olive oil and black pepper.

Teriyaki Sauce

Teriyaki Sauce can be used as a marinade for chicken, fish and lean beef strips or sirloin steak. Place chicken, fish or beef in a glass dish and pour marinade over it. To marinate chicken or beef, cover and refrigerate overnight. To marinate fish, cover and refrigerate for 1 hour. Also use Teriyaki Sauce as a basting sauce while cooking poultry and seafood.

60 ml (4 tbsp) olive oil
60 ml (4 tbsp) light soy sauce
60 ml (4 tbsp) pineapple sauce
30 ml (2 tbsp) wine vinegar
5ml (1 tsp) ground ginger
30 ml (2 tbsp) chopped spring onions
1 clove garlic, crushed
15 ml (1 tbsp) dry sherry

1. Combine ingredients in a jar and shake energetically until well combined.
2. Pour over chicken or fish.

serves 4 (125 ml/4 fl oz each)

Q

preparation time

10 minutes + marinating time

nutrient analysis

Calories per serving: 145
Protein: 2 gm
Carbohydrates: 4.4 gm
Dietary fibre: 0.05 gm
Cholesterol: 0 mg
Total fat: 13.5 gm (122 cal)
Sat fat: 1.9 gm (17 cal)
Poly fat: 1.2 gm (11 cal)
Mono fat: 9.9 gm (90 cal)

Hawaiian Marinade

This marinade gives a Polynesian flavour to chicken, fish or ribs.

1×376-g (14-oz) can crushed pineapple in natural juice
125 ml (4 fl oz) light soy sauce
60 ml (4 tbsp) olive oil
60 ml (4 tbsp) ground ginger

1. In a glass bowl, mix pineapple and soy sauce with a fork or wire whisk.
2. Whisk in the olive oil and ginger.

serves 8 (125 ml/4 fl oz each)

Q

preparation time

10 minutes

nutrient analysis

Calories per serving: 49
Protein: 0.9 gm
Carbohydrates: 4.3 gm
Dietary fibre: 0.5 gm
Cholesterol: 0 mg
Total fat: 3.4 gm (30 cal)
Sat fat: 0.5 gm (4 cal)
Poly fat: 0.3 gm (3 cal)
Mono fat: 2.5 gm (23 cal)

Sesame Marinade for Fish

serves 4 (45 ml/3 tbsp each)

Q

preparation time

10 minutes

nutrient analysis

Calories per serving: 156
Protein: 1.5 gm
Carbohydrates: 3.9 gm
Dietary fibre: 0.05 gm
Cholesterol: 0 mg
Total fat: 15.7 gm (141 cal)
Sat fat: 1.9 gm (17 cal)
Poly fat: 1.1 gm (10 cal)
Mono fat: 10 gm (90 cal)

Use this marinade for fish fillets or kebabs.

60 ml (4 tbsp) olive oil
75 ml (5 tbsp) lemon juice
15 ml (1 tbsp) lemon rind
15 ml (1 tbsp) light soy sauce
5 ml (1 tsp) honey
30 ml (2 tbsp) toasted sesame seeds
30 ml (2 tbsp) chopped fresh parsley

1. Combine olive oil, lemon juice, lemon rind, soy sauce and honey with a fork or wire whisk.
2. Whisk in sesame seeds and parsley.

Mexican Marinade for Beef

serves 4 (60 ml/4 tbsp each)

Q

preparation time

10 minutes

nutrient analysis

Calories per serving: 132
Protein: 0.3 gm
Carbohydrates: 3.2 gm
Dietary fibre: 0.3 gm
Cholesterol: 0 mg
Total fat: 13.5 gm (122 cal)
Sat fat: 1.9 gm (17 cal)
Poly fat: 1.2 gm (10 cal)
Mono fat: 10 gm (90 cal)

This spicy marinade can be poured over lean steak. Marinate steak overnight and grill.

60 ml (4 tbsp) olive oil
60 ml (4 tbsp) orange juice
60 ml (4 tbsp) tomato juice
60 ml (4 tbsp) lime juice
5 ml (1 tsp) paprika
5 ml (1 tsp) cumin
5 ml (1 tsp) dried oregano
2.5 ml (1/2 tsp) crushed dried chillies
1 clove garlic, crushed

1. Combine olive oil, orange juice, tomato juice and lime juice. Mix with a fork or wire whisk.
2. Whisk in remaining ingredients.

Wine Marinade for Lamb

Marinate lamb for dishes such as souvlakia overnight in this lemon-and-wine-flavoured marinade.

60 ml (4 tbsp) olive oil
125 ml (4 fl oz) lemon juice
60 ml (4 tbsp) dry white wine
1.25 ml (¹/₄ tsp) dried thyme
1.25 ml (¹/₄ tsp) dried rosemary
1.25 ml (¹/₄ tsp) dried oregano
1 bay leaf
2 cloves garlic, crushed
1.25 ml (¹/₄ tsp) black pepper

1. Combine olive oil, lemon juice and white wine. Mix with a fork or wire whisk.
2. Whisk in remaining ingredients.

serves 4 (60 ml/4 tbsp each)

Q

preparation time

10 minutes

nutrient analysis

Calories per serving: 138
Protein: 0.2 gm
Carbohydrates: 2.6 gm
Dietary fibre: 0.1 gm
Cholesterol: 0 mg
Total fat: 13.5 gm (122 cal)
Sat fat: 1.9 gm (69 cal)
Poly fat: 1.2 gm (11 cal)
Mono fat: 10 gm (90 cal)

Pestos and Rouilles

Pesto Sauces

Pesto sauce, an Italian creation, is a thick sauce or paste of herbs, garlic, cheese, nuts and olive oil. Pesto means pounded, and the ingredients in pesto are pounded or blended until they become a sauce. Learning to make and enjoy pesto sauces is an easy, delicious and practical way to incorporate olive oil into your diet. While classic pesto sauce is made with fresh basil, other fresh herbs are often used as well. When fresh herbs are seasonally unavailable, dried herbs can be substituted. Vegetables such as spinach, curly parsley, flat Italian parsley, coriander and watercress can also become pesto bases.

Prepared pestos can be purchased, but because they are so flavourful and simple to make, we highly recommend making your own.

Tips on making and using pestos

* Pesto can be made by hand using a mortar and pestle or in your food processor or blender. Our recipes suggest using a blender, but they will work equally well with the mortar and pestle method.

* You can keep home-made pesto in the refrigerator for 3 or 4 weeks. Pack it into a small plastic container and cover it with a thin layer of olive oil. Then tightly cover to prevent discolouring or spoiling. When you are ready to use it, you may notice some slight discoloration on the surface, but this won't harm the flavour. Stir the discoloured top layer into the rest of the pesto in the container and remove what you need. Add some more olive oil to the remaining pesto in the container, re-cover and return to the refrigerator. If you make pesto without cheese for storing and add when serving, it will keep even longer.

* Frozen pesto can be kept for 9 months. It's a good idea to freeze it in small quantities to make it easy to thaw the specific amount you need for each recipe.

* You can freeze pesto in 125 ml (4 fl oz) or 250 ml (8 fl oz) plastic containers that have tight lids. You don't need to add the layer of olive oil on top. For smaller portions, freeze pesto by the tablespoon on baking sheets covered with greaseproof paper. When the pesto ovals are frozen, transfer them to a polythene bag and fasten the top with a twist-tie to store.

* If you have fresh basil available and no time to spend in the kitchen making pesto, there's a quick alternative way to freeze it. Chop the basil and place 15 ml (1 tbsp) of chopped basil in each compartment of an ice cube tray. Then add enough olive oil to fill the trays three-quarters full. Freeze the cubes and store the frozen basil-oil blocks in a polythene bag for later use.

Quick Tips for using Pestos

1. Stuff large mushrooms with pesto, top with breadcrumbs, and place under grill until breadcrumbs are browned.

2. Use pesto as a spread for bread or baked potatoes.

3. Add pesto to soups or stews. Add to sautéed or steamed vegetable combinations.

4. Baste poultry or meat with pesto that has been thinned with basting juices and a small quantity of oil or wine.

5. Add a few tablespoons of pesto to a bread recipe to create flavourful pungent herb breads.

6. Toss your favourite cooked pasta with pesto, a little skimmed milk, and some grated Parmesan cheese.

7. Use as a basis for pasta sauce or for flavouring for dishes such as calzone or lasagne.

8. Sauté leftover seafood or poultry, steamed vegetables, and cooked rice in olive oil mixed with pesto.

9. Use as an omelette filling for omelettes made with a reduced quantity of egg yolks or egg substitute.

10. Stir 15 ml (1 tbsp) into your favourite salad dressing.

11. Top seafood or poultry with pesto before grilling.

Pine Nut Parmesan Pesto

serves 4 (60 ml/4 tbsp each)

Q

preparation time

15 minutes

nutrient analysis

Calories per serving: 339
Protein: 5 gm
Carbohydrates: 21.5 gm
Dietary fibre: 0.05 gm
Cholesterol: 0 mg
Total fat: 28.3 gm (256 cal)
Sat fat: 3.8 gm (34.5 cal)
Poly fat: 2.3 gm (20.3 cal)
Mono fat: 19.8 gm (179 cal)

50 g (2 oz) fresh basil leaves
2 cloves garlic
40 g (1¹/₂ oz) grated Parmesan cheese
30 ml (2 tbsp) grated reduced-fat Cheddar cheese
25 g (1 oz) pine nuts or walnuts
125 ml (4 fl oz) extra-virgin olive oil
freshly ground pepper

1. Purée basil, garlic, cheeses and nuts in a blender or food processor. Turn machine off, scrape sides down with a rubber spatula, and process again until well blended.
2. With machine running, slowly add olive oil in a trickle through hole in lid or feeder tube. Season with pepper to taste and process again until smooth.
3. Allow pesto to stand for 5–10 minutes before serving to allow the flavours to blend.

Variations

★ Basil Parsley Pesto: Omit cheese and nuts. Increase basil to 65 g (2¹/₂ oz). Add 15 g (¹/₂ oz) chopped fresh parsley and an additional 2 cloves garlic.
★ Mint Pesto: Omit 25 g (1 oz) basil leaves. Add 25 g (1 oz) fresh mint leaves.
★ Oregano Parsley Pesto: Omit basil leaves and reduced-fat Cheddar cheese. Add 25 g (1 oz) fresh oregano leaves and 40 g (1¹/₂ oz) fresh parsley leaves.
★ Parsley Thyme Pesto: Omit basil leaves. Add 40 g (1¹/₂oz) fresh parsley and 30 ml (2 tbsp) of dried thyme or 40 g (1¹/₂ oz) fresh parsley, 5 ml (1 tsp) dried thyme, 10 ml (2 tsp) dried rosemary and 5 ml (1 tsp) dried oregano.

Basic Rouille

Rouille is a thick, fiery Mediterranean chilli sauce that adds a new flavour dimension to soups and stews. Traditionally a diner helps himself to the rouille and swirls it into his bowl. Since rouille is very spicy, it should only be added 2.5 ml (¹/₂ tsp) at a time. It can be added to vegetable or bean soups for a memorable taste sensation.

1 red chilli (fresh or dried)
2 cloves garlic
15 ml (1 tbsp) breadcrumbs, soaked in water and pressed out
60 ml (4 tbsp) extra-virgin olive oil

1. Pound chilli and garlic in a mortar until pulverized.
2. Add breadcrumbs and slowly pour in olive oil. Mix until well blended.

serves 4 (15 ml/1 tbsp each)

Q

preparation time

15 minutes

nutrient analysis

Calories per serving: 127
Protein: 0.3 gm
Carbohydrates: 1.6 gm
Dietary fibre: 0 gm
Cholesterol: 0 mg
Total fat: 13.5 gm (122 cal)
Sat fat: 1.9 gm (16.5 cal)
Poly fat: 1.2 gm (10 cal)
Mono fat: 10 gm (89.5 cal)

Easy Blender Rouille

This is a rouille that features the added flavours of peppers and basil. It can be refrigerated for 2 or 3 weeks or frozen indefinitely.

2 small dried chillies or 5 ml (1 tsp) Tabasco sauce
¹/₂ green pepper, seeded and chopped
15 ml (1 tbsp) dried basil
3 cloves garlic, crushed
1 thick slice of white bread, crust removed, dipped in water,
*   and pressed out*
1.25 ml (¹/₄ tsp) black pepper
90 ml (6 tbsp) extra-virgin olive oil

1. If using dried peppers, blanch by placing in a bowl, pouring over boiling water to cover and allowing to stand for 5 minutes. Drain.
2. Purée chillies or Tabasco, green pepper, basil, garlic, black pepper and bread in a food processor or blender. Turn machine off, scrape sides down with a rubber spatula, and process again until well blended.
3. With machine running, slowly add olive oil in a trickle through hole in lid or feeder tube and process until smooth.

serves 18 (15 ml/1 tbsp each)

Q

preparation time

15 minutes

cooking time

5 minutes

nutrient analysis

Calories per serving: 34
Protein: 0.2 gm
Carbohydrates: 0.9 gm
Dietary fibre: 0.03 gm
Cholesterol: 0 mg
Total fat: 3.4 gm (30 cal)
Sat fat: 0.5 gm (4.5 cal)
Poly fat: 0.3 gm (2.7 cal)
Mono fat: 2.5 gm (23 cal)

Flavoured Olive Oils

Flavoured olive oils can be used in making pesto, mayonnaise and salad dressings; as a marinade for barbecued foods; in soups and stews; and as a condiment with cold seafood, poultry and vegetables.

Flavoured olive oils can be purchased commercially or you can create your own at home with any combination of fresh herbs such as basil, parsley, mint, tarragon, rosemary and thyme. Do not marinate raw garlic as it spoils easily.

Directions for Making Herb-Flavoured Olive Oil

1.   Wash and dry well 25 (1 oz) of fresh herb leaves and stems.
2.   Place the herbs in a 350 ml (12 fl oz) jar or bottle with a tight fitting lid.
3.   Fill jar or bottle with olive oil of your choice. Close tightly.
4.   Store for 3 weeks in a cool, dark place.
5.   Strain oil into another jar or bottle. Add several sprigs of fresh herbs to the oil before closing tightly. Store in refrigerator.

Also experiment with combinations of herbs as well as with lemon wedges and cloves.

Directions for Making Garlic-Pepper-Tomato-Flavoured Oil

1.   Place 15 sun-dried tomatoes (see p. 161) in a bowl and cover with warm water for 15 minutes. Drain on absorbent kitchen paper.
2.   Place half of a small crumbled dry red chilli in a small ceramic jar. Add 1 clove garlic, 1 bay leaf and 2 peppercorns. Add half the soaked tomatoes and cover with 60 ml (4 tbsp) olive oil.
3.   Add remaining crumbled chilli, 1 clove garlic, 1 bay leaf and 2 peppercorns. Fill jar with olive oil
4.   Cover and leave in a cool, dark place for at least 24 hours. Will keep for 3–4 weeks. Do not store raw garlic in oil for longer than that.

Sun-dried Tomatoes

In Italy, ripe plum tomatoes are dried in the hot sun. When dried, they look like shrivelled red chillies and are wonderfully flavourful since the drying process intensifies their natural flavour.

Sun-dried tomatoes should be used for extra flavour in a recipe instead of as a main ingredient. For example 15–30 ml (1–2 tbsp) will flavour a pasta dish for four. They can be used without additional cooking in garlicky pasta sauces, pizza, pasta salads and with strongly flavoured vegetables like broccoli or endive. They work well in stir-fries or in rice, pasta and grain salads.

Sun-dried tomatoes are sold either loose in packages or packed in oil and are quite expensive. You can make them yourself by drying the tomatoes and varying the flavourings to suit your taste, using any combination of herbs that pleases you.

During a hot, dry summer you can dry tomatoes outdoors. Otherwise, an oven will do a fine job. For the best results, you can use a home food dehydrator. This consists of several trays on which the food to be dried is stacked. Warm air is fanned through the appliance, dehydrating vegetable and fruit slices, flower heads and herbs in just a few hours.

To Dry Plum Tomatoes in the Oven:

1. Select perfect, ripe tomatoes.
2. Slice each tomato thickly and cut out any blemishes.
3. Preheat the oven to 110°C (225°F) mark ¼. Place the tomato slices on racks on baking sheets. Sprinkle tomatoes lightly with salt. Bake for 4–7 hours. Rotate baking sheets in the oven during baking time and remove slices as they dry.
4. Allow tomatoes to cool on racks.

To Dry Tomatoes for Pastas, Pizzas, Sauces or Garnishes:

1. Preheat oven to 230°C (450°F) mark 8 for 20 minutes.
2. Cut fresh red baby tomatoes in half. Grease a baking sheet with olive oil and place the tomatoes on the sheet, cut-sides up. If desired, sprinkle with herbs.
3. Place tomatoes in oven. Turn oven down to 120°C (250°F) mark ½. Leave for 2 hours or until dried to your taste.

Storing Dried Tomatoes

After tomatoes have been dried, you can store them in a herb-flavoured oil. To do this, pack dried tomatoes tightly in 250-ml (8-fl oz) jars with a layer of fresh herbs in between two layers of tomatoes. Cover with olive oil. Run a knife around the tomatoes to help air escape. Seal jars and store at room temperature for several months for best flavour.

After you've finished the tomatoes, you can reuse the remaining tomato-flavoured oil in pasta salads and for sautéeing fresh vegetables.

BREADS, BISCUITS & CAKES

Breads

Olive oil enhances and adds to the aromatic joy of baking bread from scratch. The flours and herbs added to these breads taste even better when baked with olive oil, and the loaves are fine textured and easy to cut. Almost all recipes can be adapted to include olive oil. Use the more highly flavoured oils with savoury breads such as the two herb and olive breads that follow and the milder, lighter-flavoured oils with plain or sweeter breads.

Garlic Bread

serves 8

Q

preparation time

10 minutes

cooking time

10 minutes

nutrient analysis

Calories per serving: 217
Protein: 0.05 gm
Carbohydrates: 32.3 gm
Dietary fibre: 0.9 gm
Cholesterol: 0 mg
Total fat: 7.3 gm (65 cal)
Sat fat: 0.9 gm (9 cal)
Poly fat: 0.8 gm (7 cal)
Mono fat: 5 gm (45 cal)

Here's a quick way to make your own garlic bread at home. It's the perfect accompaniment to a Greek Lentil Soup (p. 45) or Veal Stew Milano (p. 93).

1 loaf French Bread
60 ml (4 tbsp) extra-virgin olive oil
2 cloves garlic, finely crushed
1.25 ml (¼ tsp) salt (optional)

1. Preheat oven to 180°C (350°F) mark 4.
2. Split loaf in half lengthways and spread both sides with olive oil, garlic and salt, if using.
3. Put halves back together and wrap in foil.
4. Place on baking sheet and heat for 10–15 minutes until heated through.

Variation

Make 4 cm (1½ inch) diagonal slices the length of the bread but do not cut all the way through. Spread or brush garlic oil on each slice. Place, uncovered, on baking sheet and heat for 10 minutes in a preheated 180°C (350°F) mark 4 oven.

Olive Bread

This bread is made with olive oil and is full of whole olives as well. It's the perfect touch for a meal featuring a dish like Chicken Verde (p. 68) and is excellent sliced and spread with hummus or baba gannouj spread.

225 g (8 oz) strong white flour
100 g (4 oz) rye flour
10 ml (2 tsp) easy-blend dried yeast
2.5 ml (¹/₂ tsp) brown sugar
250 ml (8 fl oz) warm water
75 ml (5 tbsp) extra-virgin olive oil, plus extra for greasing
1 medium onion, finely chopped
198-g (7-oz) packet stoned green or black olives, rinsed and drained

1.   Sift white flour and rye flour into a large bowl. Stir in yeast and sugar. Make a well in the centre of the flour mixture and pour in the warm water and 30 ml (2 tbsp) of the oil. Stir to make a stiff dough. Knead on a floured surface until smooth, about 15 minutes.

2.   Wash and dry the bowl. Oil it with 15 ml (1 tbsp) of the remaining olive oil. Return dough ball to bowl and turn to coat with oil. Cover and allow to rise in a warm place until double in bulk, about 1 hour.

3.   In a small frying pan, fry onion in the remaining olive oil for 5 minutes over moderate heat until soft. Cool.

4.   Punch dough down and knead again on a well-floured surface. Work onions and whole olives into dough as you knead. Do not worry if dough seems rather moist.

5.   Oil a baking sheet or a 23-cm (9-inch) loaf tin.

6.   Shape dough into a ball and place on prepared sheet or tin. Cover and let rise again in a warm place for 1 hour.

7.   Preheat oven to 200°C (400°F) mark 6. Place loaf in oven and bake for 50 minutes–1 hour until lightly browned. Cool on wire rack.

makes 15 slices

---

preparation time

40 minutes + 2 hours rising time

---

cooking time

1 hour

---

nutrient analysis

Calories per serving: 138
Protein: 2.7 gm
Carbohydrates: 13.4 gm
Dietary fibre: 1.0 gm
Cholesterol: 0 mg
Total fat: 9.7 gm (87 cal)
Sat fat: 1.2 gm (11 cal)
Poly fat: 0.6 gm (6 cal)
Mono fat: 6.4 gm (58 cal)

Herb Bread

preparation time

50 minutes + 2 hours rising
time

cooking time

1 hour and 10 minutes

nutrient analysis

Calories per serving: 165
Protein: 4.3 gm
Carbohydrates: 25.2 gm
Dietary fibre: 1.0 gm
Cholesterol: 0.3 mg
Total fat: 5.2 gm (47 cal)
Sat fat: 0.8 gm (7.2 cal)
Poly fat: 0.4 gm (4 cal)
Mono fat: 3.6 gm (32 cal)

The International Olive Oil Council created this wonderful herb bread. Serve with Minestrone with Pesto (p. 44) or use as a base for a tuna sandwich with Cos lettuce and tomatoes.

125 ml (4 fl oz) scalded skimmed milk
75 ml (5 tbsp) extra-virgin olive oil
15 ml (1 tbsp) sugar
2.5 ml (½ tsp) salt
250 ml (8 fl oz) warm water
1 sachet active dried yeast
500 g (18 oz) strong white unbleached plain flour (or 225 g
   (8 oz) wholemeal flour and 275 g (10 oz) strong white
   flour)
100 g (4 oz) spring onions, chopped
60 ml (4 tbsp) fresh parsley
15 ml (1 tbsp) dried dill
1 clove garlic, crushed
1 egg white, lightly beaten
1.25 ml (¼ tsp) black pepper
15 ml (1 tbsp) cornflour

1.   In a small saucepan, combine milk, 30 ml (2 tbsp) of the olive oil, sugar and salt. Stir and cool until lukewarm.

2.   Place water and yeast in a large bowl. Stir. Add milk-olive oil mixture.

3.   Add 450 g (1 lb) of the flour; stir well. Add enough of remaining flour to make a stiff dough. Stir and set dough aside to rest for 10 minutes.

4.   Knead dough on a floured surface until smooth, about 15 minutes. Wash and dry the bowl. Oil it with 5 ml (1 tbsp) of the remaining olive oil. Return dough ball to bowl and turn to coat with oil. Cover and allow to rise in a warm place until double in bulk, about 1 hour.

5.   Sauté spring onions, parsley, dill and garlic in remaining olive oil for 5 minutes over moderate heat. Add beaten egg white to herb-garlic mixture. Season with pepper.

6.   Punch dough down. Turn out on to smooth surface and allow to rest for 10 minutes.

7.   Sprinkle a baking sheet with cornflour.

8.   Roll dough into rectangle 23×38 cm (9×15 inches). Spread herb-garlic filling over dough, leaving a 2.5-cm (1-inch) margin. Roll dough from narrow end, as if rolling up a Swiss roll. Pinch edges and ends of loaf to seal.

9. Transfer to baking sheet. Cover with greaseproof paper and allow to rise in a warm place until double in bulk, about 1 hour.

10. Preheat oven to 200°C (400°F) mark 6. Brush loaf with water, place in oven, and bake for 1 hour until lightly browned. Cool on wire rack.

Banana Oat Bran Muffins

This recipe has the double cholesterol-lowering ingredients of olive oil and oat bran, plus added potassium from the banana.

1 large very ripe banana
400 ml (14 fl oz) skimmed milk
75 ml (5 tbsp) mild, light-flavoured olive oil
5 ml (1 tsp) vanilla essence
40 g (1¹/₂ oz) raisins (or chopped dates)
225 g (8 oz) oat bran
15 ml (1 tbsp) baking powder
3.75 ml (³/₄ tsp) bicarbonate of soda
5 ml (1 tsp) ground cinnamon

1. Preheat oven to 200°C (400°F) mark 6. Lightly oil 12 muffin tins and dust lightly with oat bran.
2. Mash banana in a large bowl. Add milk, oil, vanilla essence and raisins and mix well with a wooden spoon.
3. Add oat bran, baking powder, bicarbonate of soda and cinnamon and mix well.
4. Fill prepared muffin tins with batter. Bake for 25 minutes until lightly browned.
5. When cool enough to touch, turn muffins out of tins on to wire racks and allow to cool. Can be stored in the refrigerator for up to 2 days, or freeze muffins and thaw as needed.

Variation
Add 1 eating apple, diced and/or 25 g (1 oz) walnuts, chopped.

makes 12

Q

preparation time

10 minutes

cooking time

25 minutes

nutrient analysis

Calories per serving: 148
Protein: 4 gm
Carbohydrates: 17.8 gm
Dietary fibre: 1.4 gm
Cholesterol: 0.6 mg
Total fat: 7.2 gm (65 cal)
Sat fat: 1.1 gm (10 cal)
Poly fat: 1 gm (9 cal)
Mono fat: 4.8 gm (43 cal)

Orange French Toast

serves 4

Q

preparation time

10 minutes + 10 minutes
soaking time

cooking time

15 minutes

nutrient analysis

Calories per serving: 465
Protein: 11.3 gm
Carbohydrates: 51 gm
Dietary fibre: 1.8 gm
Cholesterol: 137 mg
Total fat: 16.5 gm (148 cal)
Sat fat: 2.8 gm (25 cal)
Poly fat: 1.5 gm (14 cal)
Mono fat: 11.1 gm (100 cal)

Orange juice, skimmed milk and egg whites help to make this a low-cholesterol treat for a special brunch. Serve with fresh fruit, yogurt and whole-fruit jam.

250 ml (8 fl oz) orange juice
1 egg
2 egg whites
75 ml (5 tbsp) skimmed milk
5 ml (1 tsp) orange essence
30 ml (2 tbsp) sugar
1.25 ml (¼ tsp) salt (optional)
60 ml (4 tbsp) mild, light-flavoured olive oil
8 thick slices of stale bread
1 fresh orange, sliced (for garnish)

1. In a large bowl and with a wire whisk or egg beater, beat orange juice, egg, egg whites, milk, orange essence, sugar, salt, if using, and 45 ml (3 tbsp) of the olive oil until well blended.

2. Soak bread in the mixture until liquid is absorbed.

3. Heat a large frying pan with the remaining olive oil. Cook bread until lightly browned on one side, turn, and continue cooking until second side is done. Repeat until all bread is cooked. Garnish portions with orange slices.

Drop Scones and Waffles

Drop scones and waffles are light and golden when made with oats and olive oil. Serve with whole-fruit jams, yogurt and fresh fruit for a very satisfying, low-cholesterol treat.

1 whole egg
2 egg whites
350 ml (12 fl oz) skimmed milk
60 ml (4 tbsp) mild, light-flavoured olive oil
175 g (6 oz) plain flour
75 g (3 oz) quick cooking oats
15 ml (1 tbsp) baking powder
2.5 ml (¹/₂ tsp) ground cinnamon
1.25 ml (¹/₄ tsp) salt (optional)

1.   In a large bowl, mix egg, egg whites, milk and olive oil.
2.   Add flour, oats, baking powder, cinnamon and salt, if using. Mix again.
3.   Heat lightly oiled griddle, frying pan or waffle irons until hot. Pour about 125 ml (4 fl oz) batter for each waffle; about 30 ml (2 tbsp) for each drop scone. Cook drop scones until browned on one side and steam has stopped rising. Turn and cook until second side is browned. Cook waffles until lightly browned and steam has stopped rising.

serves 4

Q

preparation time

5 minutes

cooking time

10 minutes

nutrient analysis

Calories per serving: 415
Protein: 14 gm
Carbohydrates: 51.6 gm
Dietary fibre: 2.4 gm
Cholesterol: 70 mg
Total fat: 16.7 gm (150 cal)
Sat fat: 2.8 gm (25 cal)
Poly fat: 1.8 gm (16 cal)
Mono fat: 11 gm (99 cal)

Biscuits and Cakes

Olive oil can be used in a wide range of baked goods. We have included several biscuits and cakes that are low in cholesterol. Try substituting the new mild, lighter-flavoured olive oils for some or all of the fat in some of your favourite biscuit and cake recipes. These oils go very well in recipes which include fruits such as apples, oranges and bananas or which use nuts such as almonds and walnuts. Light-flavoured olive oil allows the natural flavours of the fruit and nuts to come through without smothering their taste. Baking with light-flavoured olive oil will result in smooth batters that do not leave an oily taste. Traditional muffins and drop scones are especially easy to make using olive oil, since the oil, unlike butter or margarine, does not have to be melted first but can be mixed right in. As a bonus, this also saves the melting and washing up time needed when cooking with saturated fats. Once you try these recipes, you'll want to experiment with your favourites and turn your baking into yet another way to eat healthy monounsaturated fats each day.

Sesame-Almond Biscuits

Make these sophisticated biscuits with olive oil, sesame seeds, wine, cinnamon, almonds and grated citrus rind. Here's a truly portable way to make sure you're getting your daily quota of monounsaturated olive oil.

250 ml (8 fl oz) mild, light-flavoured olive oil
5-cm (2-inch) strip lemon rind
20 ml (4 tsp) toasted sesame seeds
125 ml (4 fl oz) dry white wine
5 ml (1 tsp) grated lemon rind
5 ml (1 tsp) grated orange rind
65 g (2¹/₂ oz) sugar
50 g (2 oz) slivered almonds
400 g (14 oz) plain flour
15 ml (1 tbsp) ground cinnamon

1. Flavour oil by heating it with lemon rind and sesame seeds in a large frying pan over moderate heat. Remove from heat and cool.

2. Remove lemon rind. Pour oil and seeds into a large bowl. Add wine, grated lemon and orange rind, sugar and almonds. Stir.

3. Sift flour and cinnamon together. Add to oil mixture slowly, stirring as you proceed. Gather the dough into a ball with your hands, knead once or twice until smooth. Set aside to rest for 30 minutes.

4. Preheat oven to 180°C (350°F) mark 4. Divide dough into 18 equal pieces. Roll into a ball and flatten until biscuits are about 7.5 cm (3 inches) across and 5 mm (¹/₄ inch) thick. Bake for 20 minutes or until biscuits are lightly browned and firm. Cool on wire rack. Store in a covered container.

makes 15

preparation time

30 minutes + 30 minutes standing time

cooking time

30 minutes

nutrient analysis

Calories per biscuit: 277
Protein: 3.9 gm
Carbohydrates: 25.8 gm
Dietary fibre: 1.6 gm
Cholesterol: 0 mg
Total fat: 17.3 gm (156 cal)
Sat fat: 2.3 gm (20 cal)
Poly fat: 1.7 gm (15 cal)
Mono fat: 12.1 gm (109 cal)

Orange-Walnut Biscuits

makes 36 (2 each)

preparation time

20 minutes

cooking time

20–25 minutes

nutrient analysis

Calories per serving: 160
Protein: 2.5 gm
Carbohydrates: 14.8 gm
Dietary fibre: 0.67 gm
Cholesterol: 0 mg
Total fat: 9.9 gm (90 cal)
Sat fat: 1.3 gm (11 cal)
Poly fat: 2.1 gm (18 cal)
Mono fat: 5.9 gm (54 cal)

These light, simple, fresh orange-flavoured biscuits are crunchy and not too sweet.

50 g (2 oz) polyunsaturated margarine
125 ml (4 fl oz) mild, light-flavoured olive oil
50 g (2 oz) sugar
2.5 ml (¹/₂ tsp) ground cinnamon
2 egg whites
grated rind of 1 orange
juice of 1 orange
275 g (10 oz) plain flour (or 100 g (4 oz) wholemeal flour
*   and 175 g (6 oz) plain flour)*
7.5 ml (1¹/₂ tsp) baking powder
1.25 ml (¹/₄ tsp) salt (optional)
50 g (2 oz) walnuts, finely chopped

1. Preheat oven to 190°C (375°F) mark 5. Beat margarine with wooden spoon until creamy. Add olive oil, sugar and cinnamon and beat until well blended and fluffy.

2. Add egg, orange juice and rind and mix well.

3. Sift flour, baking powder and salt into oil mixture, adding a little at a time.

4. Add nuts and beat well.

5. Drop rounded teaspoonfuls on to un-oiled baking sheet. Bake 20–25 minutes until lightly browned. Cool on rack and store in covered container.

Rum Raisin Orange Cake

This cake is easy to make and tastes much richer than the low-cholesterol ingredients would lead you to believe. Serve it with tea or coffee.

250 ml (8 fl oz) mild, light-flavoured olive oil
175 g (6 oz) sugar
grated rind and juice of 1 lemon
grated rind and juice of 1 orange
30 ml (2 tbsp) rum (or 15 ml (1 tbsp) rum essence)
15 ml (1 tbsp) baking powder
275 g (10 oz) plain flour (preferably cake flour)
1.25 ml (¹/₄ tsp) ground cinnamon
125 g (4¹/₂ oz) raisins

1. Preheat oven to 180°C (350°F) mark 4. Lightly oil base and sides of 20-cm (8-inch) square baking tin and lightly dust with flour.

2. With a wooden spoon, beat together oil and sugar in a large bowl. Add grated lemon and orange rind. Stir in lemon and orange juice. Add rum and mix well.

3. Sift baking powder, flour and cinnamon into the oil-sugar mixture. Mix well.

4. Stir in raisins and pour mixture into prepared tin.

5. Bake for 1 hour or until lightly browned, cake has pulled away from the sides of the tin. A wooden toothpick inserted into the cake should come out clean.

serves 12

preparation time
15 minutes

cooking time
1 hour

nutrient analysis

Calories per serving: 310
Protein: 2.5 gm
Carbohydrates: 35.6 gm
Dietary fibre: 1.3 gm
Cholesterol: 0 mg
Total fat: 18.3 gm (164 cal)
Sat fat: 2.6 gm (23 cal)
Poly fat: 1.5 gm (13.5 cal)
Mono fat: 13.3 gm (119 cal)

Orange Flat Cake

serves 9

preparation time

15 minutes

cooking time

30–45 minutes

nutrient analysis

Calories per serving: 154
Protein: 2.6 gm
Carbohydrates: 22.6 gm
Dietary fibre: 0.5 gm
Cholesterol: 0.2 mg
Total fat: 6.2 gm (56 cal)
Sat fat: 0.9 gm (8 cal)
Poly fat: 0.5 gm (4.5 cal)
Mono fat: 4.4 gm (40 cal)

This moist, flat cake is based on an Italian recipe and is excellent with tea or coffee or for a light dessert.

60 ml (4 tbsp) mild, light-flavoured olive oil
100 g (4 oz) sugar
2 egg whites
100 g (4 oz) plain flour (preferably cake flour)
5 ml (1 tsp) baking powder
1.25 ml (¹/₄ tsp) salt (optional)
125 ml (4 fl oz) skimmed milk
grated rind and juice of 1 orange

1. Preheat oven to 200°C (400°F) mark 6. Lightly oil 20-cm (8-inch) square cake tin and dust lightly with flour.
2. In a large bowl, beat oil and sugar with a whisk. Add the egg whites and continue beating until well mixed.
3. Sift flour, baking powder and salt, if using, into the oil mixture. Add half of the milk and beat well. Add remaining milk and beat again.
4. Add orange juice and rind and mix.
5. Pour mixture into tin. Bake for 30–35 minutes or until lightly browned and cake has pulled away from the sides of the tin. A wooden toothpick inserted into the cake should come out clean. Leave cake in tin for 15 minutes before turning out and inverting to cool on wire rack.

Chunky Apple Cake

This spicy golden brown cake is full of apple chunks. It is perfect to take along on a picnic or for an impromptu dinner with friends.

1 whole egg
4 egg whites
100 g (4 oz) sugar
50 g (2 oz) soft light brown sugar
225 g (8 oz) plain white flour (preferably cake flour)
15 ml (1 tbsp) baking powder
5 ml (1 tsp) cinnamon
2.5 ml (¹/₂ tsp) grated nutmeg
125 ml (4 fl oz) mild, light-flavoured olive oil
675 g (1¹/₂ lb) firm apples such as granny smith, peeled, cored and cut into chunks
40 g (1¹/₂ oz) raisins
25 g (1 oz) walnuts, chopped

1. Preheat oven to 180°C (350°F) mark 4. Lightly oil a 23-cm (9-inch) square cake tin and dust with flour.

2. In a large bowl, beat egg, egg whites and sugars with a wooden spoon.

3. In a medium bowl, sift flour, baking powder, cinnamon and nutmeg. Add half of flour mixture to egg mixture. Stir in oil, then remaining flour mixture. The cake mixture will be fairly thick.

4. Fold apples, raisins and nuts into batter. Pour into prepared tin. Bake for 1 hour or until lightly browned. A wooden toothpick inserted into the cake should come out clean.

serves 9

preparation time

30 minutes

cooking time

1 hour

nutrient analysis

Calories per serving: 322
Protein: 7.4 gm
Carbohydrates: 122 gm
Dietary fibre: 2.7 gm
Cholesterol: 28.4 mg
Total fat: 16 gm (145 cal)
Sat fat: 2.6 gm (23 cal)
Poly fat: 2.2 gm (20 cal)
Mono fat: 10 gm (90 cal)

Shortcake Bases

This recipe makes wonderfully springy, easy-to-use individual shortcake bases. Top with fresh or thawed frozen strawberries, raspberries or peaches and a spoonful of low-fat yogurt.

225 g (8 oz) plain flour
15 ml (1 tbsp) baking powder
1.25 ml ($\frac{1}{4}$ tsp) salt
30 ml (2 tbsp) sugar
125 ml (4 fl oz) mild, light-flavoured olive oil
150 ml ($\frac{1}{4}$ pint) skimmed milk

1. Preheat oven to 200°C (400°F) mark 6.
2. Sift flour, baking powder, salt and sugar into a large bowl.
3. Add olive oil and milk and stir with a wooden spoon to form a ball of soft dough.
4. Knead dough about 10 times on a lightly floured surface. Roll out dough until 1 cm ($\frac{1}{2}$ inch) thick. Cut 6 or 7 rounds with a 7.5-cm (3-inch) cutter or glass, re-rolling dough scraps again and cutting rounds until you have 8 rounds.
5. Bake on ungreased baking sheet for 25–30 minutes until lightly browned. Cool on wire racks.

---

makes 8

Q

preparation time

15 minutes

cooking time

20–25 minutes

nutrient analysis

Calories per serving: 245
Protein: 3.7 gm
Carbohydrates: 26 gm
Dietary fibre: 0.8 gm
Cholesterol: 0.8 mg
Total fat: 14 gm (126 cal)
Sat fat: 2.1 gm (19 cal)
Poly fat: 1.5 gm (14 cal)
Mono fat: 10 gm (90 cal)

Carrot Cake

This is a light version of a classic carrot cake that uses olive oil and egg whites instead of butter and whole eggs. Serve it for tea and pack any leftovers for a perfect lunchtime snack.

4 large carrots, about 575 g (1¹/₄ lb)
350 g (12 oz) plain flour or 150 g (5 oz) wholemeal flour
*   and 200 g (7 oz) plain flour*
15 ml (1 tbsp) bicarbonate of soda
15 ml (1 tbsp) mixed spice
15 ml (1 tbsp) ground cinnamon
2.5 ml (¹/₂ tsp) salt (optional)
2 whole eggs
4 egg whites
300 ml (¹/₂ pint) mild, light-flavoured olive oil
450 g (1 lb) sugar
250 ml (8 fl oz) unsweetened apple purée
15 ml (1 tbsp) vanilla essence
175 g (6 oz) sultanas
50 g (2 oz) walnuts, chopped

1. Preheat oven to 180°C (350°F) mark 4. Lightly oil a 23×33-cm (9×13-inch) cake tin, or a 23-cm (9-inch) ring tin. Lightly dust with flour.

2. Cut off ends, peel and cut carrots into 2.5-cm (1-inch) slices. Steam until soft, about 10 minutes, in steamer with 2.5 cm (1 inch) of water in tightly covered pan or cook in microwave. Purée with potato masher or in blender or food processor, pushing down carrots with a rubber spatula until well puréed.

3. In a medium bowl, sift flour, bicarbonate of soda, mixed spice, cinnamon and salt, if using, and mix well with a wooden spoon.

4. In a large bowl, with an electric or wire whisk, beat eggs, egg whites, olive oil, sugar, carrot purée, apple purée and vanilla until well mixed.

5. Add flour mixture and beat for 2–3 minutes.

6. Fold in sultanas and nuts. Pour mixture into prepared tin. Bake for 1¹/₄–1¹/₂ hours until lightly browned and cake has pulled away from sides of the tin. A wooden toothpick inserted into the cake should come out clean. Put tin on wire rack and cool for 15 minutes. If cake has been made in a Swiss roll tin, leave in tin. If a ring tin has been used invert cake on to serving plate to continue cooling.

makes 12 slices

preparation time
30 minutes

cooking time
1¹/₄ hours

nutrient analysis
Calories per serving: 360
Protein: 7.8 gm
Carbohydrates: 74 gm
Dietary fibre: 4.0 gm
Cholesterol: 93 mg
Total fat: 5.3 gm (48 cal)
Sat fat: 0.8 gm (7 cal)
Poly fat: 2.3 gm (20 cal)
Mono fat: 1.4 gm (13 cal)

Bibliography

Alabaster, Oliver. *The Power of Prevention*. New York, Simon & Schuster, 1986.

American Heart Association Nutrition Committee: Dietary Guidelines for Healthy American Adults: A Statement for Physicians and Health Professionals by the Nutrition Committee, American Heart Association. Circulation vol. 74 (1986), p. 1465A–1468A.

Aravanis, Christos, and Paul J. Ionnidis. 'Nutritional Factors and Cardio-vascular Diseases in the Greek Island Heart Study,' in *Nutritional Prevention of Cardiovascular Disease*. New York, Academic Press, 1984.

Canola Oil: Properties and Performance. Winnipeg, Canola Council, 1987.

Composition of Foods. Agricultural Handbook No. 5. United States Department of Agriculture, Washington, D.C. Government Printing Office, 1976–1986.

Cooper, Kenneth H., M.D. *Controlling Cholesterol*. New York, Bantam, 1988.

David, Elizabeth. *Classics: Mediterranean Food, French Country Cooking, Summer Cooking*. New York, Knopf, 1980.

Davidson, Alan. *Mediterranean Seafood*. New York, Penguin, 1980.

DeBakey, Michael, et al. 'Diet, Nutrition, and Heart Disease.' *Journal of the American Medical Association*, vol. 86 (1987), 729–31.

Dumas, Alexandre. *Dictionary of Cuisine*. New York, Simon & Schuster, 1958.

Goldbeck, Nikki and David. *The Goldbeck's Guide to Good Food*. New York, New American Library, 1987.

Grundy, Scott M., M.D., PhD. 'Cholesterol and Coronary Heart Disease: A New Era.' *Journal of the American Medical Association*, vol. 256 (1986), 2849–58.

Grundy, Scott M., M.D., PhD. 'Comparison of Dietary Saturated and Polyunsaturated Fatty Acids on Plasma Lipids and Lipoproteins in Man.' *Journal of Lipid Research*, vol. 26 (1985), 194–202.

Grundy, Scott M., M.D., PhD. 'Comparison of Monosaturated Fatty Acids and Carbohydrates for Plasma Cholesterol Lowering.' *New England Journal of Medicine*, vol. 314 (1986), 745–48.

Grundy, Scott M., M.D., PhD. 'Effects of Polyunsaturated Fats on Lipid Metabolism in Patients with Hypertriglyceridemia.' *Journal of Clinical Investigation*, vol. 55 (1975), 269–82.

Grundy, Scott M., M.D., PhD. 'Monosaturated Fatty Acids, Plasma Cholesterol, and Coronary Heart Disease.' *American Journal of Clinical Nutrition*, vol. 45 (1987), 1168–75.

Hodgson, Moira. *The New York Times Gourmet Shopper*. New York, Times Books, 1983.

Kennedy, Diana. *The Cuisines of Mexico*. New York, Harper & Row, 1972.

Keys, Ancel, et. al. *Seven Countries: A Multivariate Analysis of Death and Coronary Heart Disease*. Cambridge, Harvard University Press, 1980.

Klein, Maggie Blyth. *The Feast of the Olive*. Los Angeles. Aris, 1983.

Levenstein, Harvey. *Revolution at the Table: The Transformation of the American Diet*. New York, Oxford University Press, 1988.

McConnell, Carol and Malcolm. *The Mediterranean Diet*. New York, W. W. Norton and Company, 1987.

National Institutes of Health Consensus Conference. 'Lowering Blood Cholesterol to Prevent Heart Disease.' *Journal of the American Medical Association*, vol. 253 (1985), 2080–90.

Nutritive Value of American Foods, Agricultural Handbook No. 456. United States Department of Agriculture, Washington, D.C., Government Printing Office, 1975.

Olney, Richard. *Simple French Food*. New York, Atheneum, 1974.

Rinzler, Carol Ann. *The Complete Food Book*. New York, World Almanac, 1987.

Roden, Claudia. *A Book of Middle Eastern Food*. New York, Vintage, 1974.

Root, Waverly. *The Food of France*. New York, Random House, 1958.

Root, Waverly. *The Food of Italy*. New York, Random House, 1971.

Simone, Charles B. *Cancer and Nutrition*. New York, McGraw-Hill, 1983.

Thomas, Briony. *Meat Diet and Health, a Report on Red Meat Today*. Meat and Livestock Commission with the Health Education Authority, 1990.

Viola, Publio, and Audisio, Mirella. *Olive Oil and Health: A Research Compendium*. Crete, International Congress on the Biological Value of Olive Oil, 1986.

Visser, Margaret. *Much Depends on Dinner*. New York, Grove Press, 1987.

Vitale, J. J., and Broitman, S. A. 'Lipids and the Immune Function.' *Cancer Research*, vol. 41 (1981), 3706.

Von Welanetz, Diana and Paul. *The Von Welanetz Guide to Ethnic Ingredients*. Los Angeles, J. P. Tarcher Inc., 1982.

Wolfert, Paula. *Mediterranean Cooking*. New York, Times Books, 1977.

Index